METHUEN
SCREENPLAY

Stephen Poliakoff

SHE'S BEEN AWAY
& HIDDEN CITY

She's Been Away & Hidden City

She's Been Away will be shown by BBC television in the autumn of this year with Peggy Ashcroft playing Lillian.

'*Hidden City* works with tremendous effectiveness as both urban thriller and political metaphor. At the heart of both is the English obsession with secrecy . . . holds one spellbound . . .'
Alexander Walker, Evening Standard

'Poliakoff's view of London is almost like a ghostly and sensuous excavation. The film inhabits underground tunnels, waste tips and wartime shelters as eloquently as it moves around its streets and buildings. Physically it is a fascinating progress and one which very neatly dovetails with Poliakoff's open attack on a society which permits its bureaucrats so many official secrets.'
Derek Malcom, The Guardian

'A directorial debut by a leading playwright and screenwriter in a fascinating tale for paranoid city dwellers.'
The Sunday Times

'Superb . . . The sort of movie that ensures you never feel secure walking the streets again.'
Steve Grant, Time Out

STEPHEN POLIAKOFF, born in 1952, was appointed Writer in Residence at the National Theatre for 1976 and the same year won the Evening Standard's Most Promising Playwright award for *Hitting Town* and *City Sugar*. He also won a BAFTA Award for the Best Single Play of 1980 for *Caught on a Train*. His plays and films include *Clever Soldiers* (1974), *The Carnation Gang* (1974), *Hitting Town* (1975), *City Sugar* (1975), *Heroes* (1975), *Strawberry Fields* (1977), *Stronger than the Sun* (1977), *Shout Across the River* (1978), *American Days* (1979), *The Summer Party* (1980), *Bloody Kids* (1980), *Caught on a Train* (1980), *Favourite Nights* (1981), *Soft Targets* (1982), *Runners* (1983), *Breaking the Silence* (1984), and *Coming in to Land* (1987).

STEPHEN POLIAKOFF

She's Been Away
&
Hidden City

METHUEN DRAMA

A METHUEN SCREENPLAY

First published as a paperback original in Great Britain 1989
by Methuen Drama, Michelin House, 81 Fulham Road, London SW3 6RB
and distributed in the United States by HEB Inc, 70 Court Street,
Portsmouth, New Hampshire 03801

Photographs from the film of *She's Been Away* taken by Dave Green and
Gary Williamson
Photography copyright © 1989 BBC

Photographs from the film *Hidden City* taken by David Farrell
Photography copyright © 1989 Film on Four

Printed in Great Britain
A CIP Catalogue record for this book is available from The British
Library.

Printed and bound in Great Britain by
Cox & Wyman Ltd, Reading

She's Been Away

THE CAST

She's Been Away first broadcast by BBC-TV in autumn 1989.

LILLIAN	Peggy Ashcroft
HARRIET	Geraldine James
HUGH	James Fox
DOMINIC	Jackson Kyle
YOUNG LILLIAN	Rebecca Pidgeon
GLADYS	Rosalie Crutchley
MATILDA	Rachel Kempson
GEORGE	Hugh Lloyd
NURSE, *(Mental Hospital)*	Brid Brennan
DOCTOR *(Mental Hospital)*	David Hargreaves
LOUISE	Robyn Moore
HARLEY STREET DOCTOR	Richard Haddon Haines
YOUNG COUSIN EDWARD	Barnaby Holm
YOUNG LILLIAN'S FATHER	Donald Douglas
CITY FRIEND AT PARTY	Malcolm Mudie
MOVIE BUFF	David Timson
SUPERMARKET CASHIER	Anne Haydn
TRAFFIC WARDEN	Doyle Richmond
WOMAN IN HOSPITAL RECEPTION	Maureen Nelson
VICAR	Roger Davidson
YOUNG DOCTOR *(Baby Scan)*	Richard Huw
HOTEL RECEPTION CLERK	Jon Strickland
POLICEMAN IN NEWS ITEM	Nick Kemp
HEAD WAITER	Michael Carter
MAN AT DANCE	David Pullan
HOTEL PARTY GUEST	Graham Callan
YOUNG WOMAN AT RECEPTION	Claire Williamson
DOCTOR *(Country Hospital)*	James Griffiths
NURSE *(Country Hospital)*	Francesca Buller
1920'S DOCTOR	Hugh Ross
DIRECTOR	Peter Hall
PRODUCER	Kenith Trodd
DESIGNER	Gary Williamson
COSTUME DESIGNER	Anushia Nieradzik
LIGHT CAMERAMAN	Philip Bonham-Carter
EDITOR	Ardan Fisher

The Young Lillian (Rebecca Pidgeon) in the hospital

Lillian (Peggy Ashcroft) among the flowers
celebrating Harriet's pregnancy

Gladys
(Rosalie Crutchley)
and Matilda
(Rachel Kempson)
at the funeral

Hugh
(James Fox)
and Harriet
(Geraldine James)
at the scan

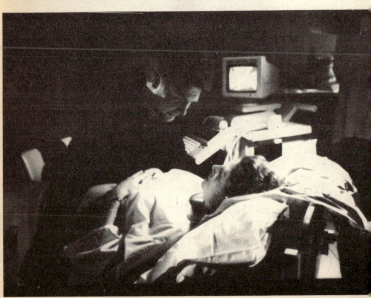

Harriet in the hotel restaurant at the end of the meal with Lillian

Dominic (Jack Kyle) gives advice to his father
on whether to pay a ransom

Lillian sees the two brothers at the party
and begins to remember the past

Opening Title Sequence – Interior Mental Hospital – Day

The camera moves very slowly across a series of objects underneath the titles – old shoes, a model of St. Paul's Cathedral, some china figurines, covered in dust. They are evocative and strange.

Exterior: The Driveway; Mental Hospital – Day

A car approaches down a long drive, a silver Daimler passing ill-kept rhododendron bushes and piles of autumn leaves being burnt. Through the windscreen we see a large, shambling Victorian building.

HUGH *is driving, he leans purposefully over the wheel. A man in his late thirties, he has a good natured face, exudes confidence, genial certainty. Next to him, HARRIET is smoking, looking at the great decaying building coming into view. She is in her mid-thirties, and is expensively, fashionably dressed. She has a sharp, ironic manner.*

Exterior: Mental Hospital: Entrance – Day

They reach the building through a fog of builders' dust. As they get out of the car, sofas, chairs, boxes, old carpets, are being thrown from a first floor window down into a massive skip. From several other windows roundabout in the building, pale faces stare down, mostly old people, one or two much younger. They watch carefully as HARRIET and HUGH get out of the car.

HARRIET (*almost being hit by the builders as she climbs out of the car*). This can't be the right place, can it?

HUGH. Of course it is. How could I come to the wrong place? I've been here before.

HARRIET *watches the faces staring out of the window, through the haze of builders' dust. One of the builders has a radio blasting out Radio One, as they chuck the contents of the building out.*

HUGH. Do you think I should take the chair? (*He is fiddling with a shiny new wheelchair from the boot of the car.*) I don't know if she needs it, it may not be the thing to do . . .

HARRIET. How do I know what the thing to do is. . . ? Let's get it over.

HUGH (*decisively, straightening out wheelchair*). I'll take it – she might appreciate it.

Interior: Old Mental Hospital: Corridor – Day

A NURSE *is heading down a passage clouded with builders' dust, leading* HARRIET *and* HUGH. *The* NURSE *is walking very fast,* HUGH *pushing the empty wheelchair racing along, and* HARRIET *half having to run to keep up with them.*

NURSE. There's no easy way of doing this, no rules, there's almost nothing you can do wrong in these circumstances . . . or right for that matter.

HUGH. Yes, it's not exactly the sort of thing you do everyday! Collecting somebody who's been shut up for –

NURSE (*cutting him off*). But don't expect reactions. She's a very docile sort of person, passive creature now, she could have been let out of here a long time ago really.

HUGH. I know, my mother wouldn't try to get her out. . . (*Hurrying after the* NURSE.) my mother's dead now, so –

NURSE (*cutting in*). Don't expect her to respond at all, she doesn't really understand anything that's going on round here, just wants to be on her own.

They have come to a barrier in the passage, a makeshift wooden barrier, that they have to get through and squeeze the wheelchair through.

The NURSE *guides an old man who's got through the barrier and is glancing around the doorway, back into his part of the building.*

This is meant to keep them out of the builders' way. (*To old man.*) But some of us get through don't we?. . . (*Firmly to old man.*) I don't know why, because there's nothing to see.

HARRIET (*squeezing last through the barrier*). You seem to be knocking the place down around them –

NURSE. There's a deadline by which time the building has to be empty. So they had to start on this wing – nothing we could do.

Interior: Mental Hospital: Ballroom – Day

Cut to the NURSE, HUGH and HARRIET crossing a large room, like an old ballroom, now full of split leather armchairs and a central table completely covered in belongings, old clothes, shoes, handbags, old pocket mirrors, hats. Several of the inmates are sitting round the room in corners, peering through the dust filled air, for the builders' dust has permeated into this part of the building.

We can see workmen and builders' machinery outside the window of the ballroom.

NURSE (*marching across the room indicating the people in the shadows as she moves*). All of these will be leaving in the next three months, they all have to be gone by then. (*She points to an old man in the corner sitting alone.*) That's George, used to spend a lot of time with your Aunt once, but I haven't seen them near each other for several years.

HARRIET *stops by the table of belongings, as the NURSE begins to sweep on.*

Those are all belongings of people that died here, over the years. (*Pointing at the inmates.*) We're trying to encourage any of these to take what they want – some of them may really need it. . (*She smiles pleasantly at one of them.*) It's their own antiques road show, isn't it? (*Sharp.*) Come on, the doctor's waiting.

HARRIET *is staring at the evocative spread of belongings including small china figures, some of them quite beautiful.*

HUGH *moves up to the belongings breezily, pleasant smile.*

HUGH. Isn't it odd what some people want to keep. Careful darling, we don't want to break anything.

NURSE (*not unkindly*). Anything you want – just grab it. We've got literally rooms full of that stuff.

Interior: Mental Hospital: Corridor – Day

HUGH *and* HARRIET *sitting obediently on very low chairs in the passage, as a DOCTOR holding a file leans against a door opposite them. The NURSE is also there. The DOCTOR is leafing through the*

*file and swinging on the door. As he swings on the door, they can just
catch a glimpse of an old lady sitting with her back to them in the far
room.*

*Next to them in the passage is a line of three fish tanks, full of weeds,
dark green water, but still with quite large fish in them.*

HUGH (*pleasant smile*). I remember the fish from last time.

DOCTOR. Yes, we tried to brighten the place up. (*He glances at
the dark fish.*) But we seem to have all lost interest after a time,
didn't we . . . when we knew the building was going. (*The*
DOCTOR *gently swings on the door.*) She won't remember your
last visit.

HUGH. I know.

HARRIET *is looking at the dishevelled paper chains and other
efforts to brighten the place up, now shrivelled. There are also some
paintings and drawings stuck on the wall further down the passage.*
HARRIET*'s gaze settles on a striking almost cartoon version of a
middle aged man's head.*

DOCTOR. She doesn't remember anything, but you'll find she's
very easy. She likes doing her own cooking . . . that was a new
development about 10 years ago, simple things like sausages,
scrambled egg. She never watches TV, she's in a totally
insulated world, in fact, very little, if anything, gets through. . .

HARRIET *finds she's staring through the crack of the door at the
back of the old lady, and then at the strange shaped fish right beside
her in the tank.*

You have to remember she's been in institutions for over sixty
years, there's not much left when that's happened.

HUGH (*earnestly*). Of course, I meant to do this gradually, take
her out to tea, on trips, have her come to stay for weekends, but
with you closing her ward, it –

DOCTOR (*pleasantly*), Yes, yes. It wouldn't have made any
difference. Good. (*He closes the file.*) She's all yours. Take care
of her, don't let her out of the house on her own, that sort of
thing. Use your common sense (*he smiles straight at them*) which
I'm sure you possess. Otherwise she'll be as good as gold, won't

she sister? (*He begins to move off down passage, then turns, pleasantly.*) I'm getting my release too this week, early retirement (*as if answering an enquiry from them*) mixed feelings, really – (*he smiles*) but basically I can't wait.

Interior: Mental Hospital: Ward – Day

LILLIAN *sitting in the foreground of shot in deep old chair, alone, right close to the window overlooking a courtyard. As she senses them approaching, she closes her eyes.*

NURSE. Have you got everything now Lillian? (LILLIAN's *eyes still shut.*) We packed, didn't we. Come on, you are not really asleep are you? It's the day we've been waiting for.

There are two old battered suitcases, with Lillian's name written on them in girlish handwriting, standing among the empty beds in the wards. Some of the beds have already been stripped of their mattresses.

HUGH (*crouching down by* LILLIAN *so his head is close to hers*). Aunt Lillian – we've come to take you home. Do you remember me? . . . Hugh, Margaret's son, I've been before to –

HARRIET (*turning away, staring about the empty ward*). She doesn't remember, Hugh, they told us.

LILLIAN *staring straight back at* HUGH.

LILLIAN. Is he here to clean? I'll move then, if he's going to clean.

NURSE. Don't be silly – it's your big day today.

LILLIAN (*to* HARRIET). Have you got some clean sheets at last? (*Sharp.*) Have you brought them? You can make my bed then.

HARRIET. I'm Harriet. Hugh's wife. I've come to . . . (*she stops, embarrassed*) help on the journey (*she smiles*) be in the way.

LILLIAN *stares back at her, there is something direct and unsettling in her look,* HARRIET *moves, glances out of the window at the view* LILLIAN *has been staring at. The window overlooks a grubby courtyard, with a large white tiled wall directly opposite. The courtyard is full of old pieces of furniture and other junk.*

NURSE (*in background of shot, as* HARRIET *is looking*). Say goodbye to your seat Lillian – this is where she's spent years just sitting. Only wants to look at the wall, quite happy if she can do that. (*Warmly.*) Silly girl, it's not the best view around here.

HARRIET (*staring right down into the bottom of the courtyard*). Jesus, what a dump.

Interior: Mental Hospital: Corridor – Day

The NURSE, HUGH *and* HARRIET *move along the long passage with* LILLIAN. HUGH *pushing* LILLIAN *in the wheelchair,* HARRIET *carrying the suitcases.* LILLIAN *is clasping a small bag. They pass through the barrier.*

LILLIAN. We are going the wrong way. I'm not meant to be going this way! This is not right!

NURSE. I've been telling you for weeks Lillian, come on now. You are going outside.

LILLIAN. I'm going to walk. Let me walk. (*She gets out of the wheelchair, she stays close to the wall. Sharp, to* HUGH.) You don't know where you're going do you?

Interior/Exterior: Mental Hospital: Entrance – Day

Cut to LILLIAN *standing facing the large main door. The camera is behind her, as the door opens, and she steps out. A wall of dust greets her and the builders standing on top of the great pile of rubble and junk already filling the drive, seen from* LILLIAN's *point of view, look strange and slightly threatening. All round the building, faces are staring from windows, as some of the remaining inmates watch her.*

HUGH (*taking her by the arm*). This way, this is the car. (*Gently.*) You don't mind riding in one of those do you? Let's sit in the front.

LILLIAN *tenses slightly at the sight of the car. She lets herself be put in the car, but she insists on the back seat, automatically moving there, she is not looking at anyone.*

Exterior: Mental Hospital/Interior: Car – Day

The car moves off, HUGH *glancing at her in the mirror, as she sits on the back seat.*

HUGH (*slowly, as if to a child*). When was the last time you went outside? (*Gently.*) When you were outside the home?

LILLIAN *seeming not to listen, she is staring back at the receding view of the home, the large Victorian building, gradually disappearing behind trees.*

HARRIET. She hasn't been out for a long time we know that, the doctor said –

HUGH (*firmly*). Yes, but I want to know how long.

LILLIAN *has suddenly started burrowing among her belongings in the bag she is clasping, hunting furiously for something.*

LILLIAN (*Loud*). Stop. Stop it. (*Catching the door handle as car is moving.*) Stop at once . . . stop it.

HUGH *brakes sharply, they have just turned onto the main road.* LILLIAN *very agitated, searching.*

I lost it.

HUGH *gets out, leans through the back door to help her.*

HUGH. Now, it's alright Lillian. Calm down, tell me slowly, what have you lost?

He starts going through the belongings, a seemingly random selection, in bag. Slow tone.

The apple is here, that's not it is it? The gloves . . . the tin plate? Not that? Your greeting cards, and this old picture book, that's not it is it?

LILLIAN *suddenly looks relieved. She's holding a pair of silver sugar tongs, now freckled with black.*

Is that what it was? Those tongs. Hold onto them now. Everything OK? . . .

HARRIET *whispers to him as he climbs back into the driving seat.*

HARRIET. We haven't even *started* Hugh . . . it's too sudden doing it this way, it's crazy, I don't think she's ready for it. (*Even quieter.*) *I'm* not anyway.

HUGH (*reassuring, confident*). Everything's under control now . . . sit back and relax Lillian. We can all enjoy the drive, lots to see.

HARRIET (*sharp smile to* LILLIAN). He'll call out some of the sights I expect.

Exterior: London Suburbs/Interior: Car

Vivid shots of coming in to London, motorways, large vehicles, juggernauts, speeding coaches, past the airport, with a 747 coming in to land, very low, seemingly about to scrape the tops of houses, a huge DIY store in the middle of a traffic interchange, pylons marching across the landscape, and then sudden unfamiliar palm trees clustering round a mosque in Surrey with its golden dome shining in the sun.

HARRIET. Have we got lost? This doesn't look right at all. We're going round in circles Hugh!

And then onto LILLIAN's *eyes, a distant stare, confused by all she sees outside the window, she looks away, shutting it out, starts scrabbling amongst her things.*

Exterior: Street Outside London House – Day

The car rounding the corner into leafy residential street in Holland Park.

HUGH. This is it Lillian. We're home. Do you remember this street? Do you recognise the houses? There's the family house! It's still the same one you were brought up in.

LILLIAN *is not looking, staring down at her things.*

The door knob! Remember the door knob?

There is a striking door knob of a lion's head on the door of a substantial early Victorian house, set back from the road.

LILLIAN *looks up for a second.*

HARRIET. Leave her alone.

LILLIAN (*pulling her belongings close to her*). I don't know why you've brought me here. I'm going to be late back. You're going to get me into trouble because of this.

Interior: London House: Hall – Day

Subjective shot as LILLIAN *enters the house. Her point of view moving into the hall, as a small reception party stands waiting for her. A young English nanny,* LOUISE, *and a Portuguese cook,* THERESA, *are standing with an eight year old boy* DOMINIC. LILLIAN *is looking neither left or right.*

HUGH's *voice cutting into her point of view.*

This is my son, Dominic and Louise who looks after him . . . and Theresa, Lillian, where you going?

LILLIAN *not stopping, moving slowly but purposefully, ignoring everyone.*

Things have changed of course since you'll remember the house, but there's still a lot the same. Your rooms are through here, in the new extension –

A small frisson crosses LILLIAN's *face as she moves past some pictures, portraits of relatives, but we can't tell if she has recognized anything or just uneasy with her surroundings. She shuffles out of the hall.*

LILLIAN (*muttering*). This is all wrong . . . you've brought me to the wrong place.

Interior: London House: Granny Flat – Day

HUGH *guides her through the large house to a self-contained granny flat at the back.*

HUGH (*gently enthusiastic*). This is your flat, you see completely self-contained, bathroom . . . what estate agents would call luxury kitchen, small but it's got everything, and there's food in the fridge, patio out there. (*Correcting himself, in case she's unfamiliar with the term.*) Little paved garden, it's about 20′ by 20′, you can sit out there . . . flowers from the garden.

LILLIAN *has been standing in the middle of the bedroom while he's been saying this, a look of incomprehension in her eyes. She picks up some of the flowers out of the vase.*

LILLIAN (*holding the flowers*). When do you come in here to clean?

HUGH (*patient smile*). I told you I don't clean – but if you want it cleaned, I think it's spotless, but –

LILLIAN. If you clean it *now*, I can have my rest.

HUGH. It *has* been cleaned.

LILLIAN (*pushing the flowers at him*). Take the flowers, I'm not allowed any flowers.

HUGH (*slowly*). You are here now, this is home, there are no rules.

LILLIAN. And I'm not allowed two pillows (*handing him pillows*) and these are breakable, I'm not allowed them, take them away. (*Indicating china ornaments.*)

HUGH'*s arms are now full. Piled high, from things to remove.* LILLIAN *staring at him.*

How much time is there left now?

HUGH. Time till when?

LILLIAN *looks cross at him not understanding.*

LILLIAN. Time till you have to switch off all the lights of course.

Interior: Dining Room – Evening

HUGH, HARRIET *and* DOMINIC *are sitting round the dinner table, staring at the celebratory meal prepared for* LILLIAN, *a fine fresh salmon lies in front of them, and some beautifully prepared salads. Candles are flickering on the table. They are eyeing the empty chair at the head of the table.*

HUGH. We were told this would happen . . . take no notice. She'll come when she's ready. We *must* leave her alone.

DOMINIC *is twisting his chair, staring down the passage that leads off the dining room. There is a curl of smoke visible, coming from round the corner.*

DOMINIC. There's a terrible smell. Can't you smell it? It's horrible. . . (*He twists round.*) It's disgusting.

HARRIET. Dominic you always state the obvious – just eat up, and keep quiet.

HARRIET *though is also eyeing the passage, where the smoke is visible.*

DOMINIC. If she sets the house on fire, will they blame you? (*He looks confidently at* HUGH.) Are we insured for any damage she does?

Interior: Granny Flat – Night

Cut to the interior of the little kitchen, LILLIAN *with grilled sardines, smoking, burnt. She is just taking them off the grill, and putting them on a tin plate, the same tin plate we saw in the car.*

We see LILLIAN *staring down at the modern gadgets, waste disposal, coffee maker, Magimix, that* HUGH *has put in the little kitchen for her. A moment of her alone among the alien machinery, touching it.*

Then we cut to her sitting alone in her room, eating off her tin plate on her knees, determinedly.

We see that her room is now completely empty, except for the bed, and the chair, and her two suitcases.

Interior: Main Bedroom – Night

HUGH *and* HARRIET *lying in bed, it is dark.*

Close up of HARRIET *as she lies there, wide awake. There is a strange noise from downstairs, something rhythmically banging, again and again, like something knocking against a pipe or a radiator.*

HARRIET. Do you hear that?

HUGH. Of course I hear that. (*The knocking is even louder.*) It's Lillian, naturally.

HARRIET. The whole street must be able to hear. They'll think we've got a trapped animal in the house, or something.

HUGH (*switching on side light*). It's OK. The first night was always going to be difficult.

HARRIET (*quiet*). It's not OK . . . I don't want her breaking anything down there.

HUGH. We just couldn't put her straight in another home, without her having a chance to see outside. I feel very strongly about that, don't you? (*With feeling.*) She is family after all. Anyway Aunt Sarah said she would have her next year, when she's finished the conversion in her basement. Its only for a little while darling . . .

Close up of HARRIET *as the unsettling noise continues, in fact seems to be getting louder.*

HARRIET. This isn't going to work Hugh. (*Quiet.*) There isn't a chance in hell.

Interior: Granny Flat – Night

We see LILLIAN *from the back. She is sitting up in the dark room on single chair, rocking backwards and forwards, banging her radiator with her tin plate, not in a desperate fashion, more as if she's just occupying the time. We move closer to her, as she sways on the chair.*

Exterior: London Street – Night.

Shot down into the street, the night world LILLIAN *is staring at. We see two kids riding by on bicycles covered in luminous lights, glowing back at* LILLIAN.

We cut back to LILLIAN's *face.*

Then back into the street, a car draws up, its engine running very loudly, doors slamming, loud Kensington voices shouting in the night streets, oblivious.

We cut back to LILLIAN *swaying in her chair.*

Interior: Main Drawing Room – Day

Bright sunlight in the main drawing room. LILLIAN *is sitting bolt upright in a chair facing* HUGH *who is just completing drawing a family tree on a blackboard.* LILLIAN*'s demeanour is peaceful, but totally impassive, one can't tell if she's taking in a single thing* HUGH *is saying. But her eyes are very watchful.*

HUGH *making a scratching noise with the chalk as he completes the diagram.*

HUGH. I haven't written on a blackboard for some time, forgive the squeak. NOW, Lillian. (*He points to the top of the family tree.*) This is Grandfather Edwin sitting up here, he had two children, one of whom was your father, Gerald, he married Letticia, your mother, you see I've underlined them in red, can you see that?

LILLIAN *watching but not responding.*

And there were eight children, yes eight. You were fifth, my mother third, can you remember your sister Margaret? My mother? (*Curious.*) Got any feeling about her?

HUGH *is using his patient slow tone, as if to a small girl. He spreads some photos in front of* LILLIAN *on the table.*

(*Sitting opposite her at the gleaming mahogany table.*) Can you pick out the photo of you as a young girl?

LILLIAN *surveys the pictures, her hand moving over them for a moment, hovering. Then, like a small child, as if taking her cue from his tone of voice, she flicks the pictures onto the floor.*

(*Watching her closely.*) You don't remember anything do you? (HUGH *takes her by the hand, looking very directly.*) Do you like to be called Lillian or *Lilly*? They used to call you Lilly as a girl, didn't they? (*He calls her name.*) Lilly? Lillian? (*Decides on Lilly*). Lilly.

LILLIAN (*staring straight back at him*). Can I go to my room now? I don't think I'm allowed out of the room for this long.

HUGH. I told you you can do whatever you like now, Lilly.

LILLIAN (*sharply*). And there is no pot under my bed . . . it's been forgotten.

HUGH (*smiling*). I'll see to that.

HARRIET *is standing watching from the stairs.*

(*Turns.*) She doesn't remember anything, they were right.

HARRIET. We know that for chrissake. And stop drawing her diagrams, she's not come here to be made to work. Have you?

LILLIAN *and* HARRIET's *eyes meet.* HARRIET *disconcerted by her look.*

Interior: Harley Street Consulting Room – Day

HARRIET *lying prone, her face in close up, her dress rolled up, as she's examined out of frame. We stay on her face, she's rolling her eyes with impatience.*

DOCTOR. Everything's fine. In spanking order.

We see him, moving over to desk, fine Harley Street interior. He is about 40, but seems older.

HARRIET. You took your time – I thought you'd got lost down there.

DOCTOR (*sitting down at desk*). We have to be thorough naturally, when –

HARRIET. When the mother-to-be is as ancient as this one you mean.

HARRIET *lights a cigarette.*

DOCTOR. No, no, plenty of time for you to have at least four more.

HARRIET *looks horrified, blows smoke.*

HARRIET. What a terrifying thought. (*She takes an ostentatious drag, as if daring him to tell her to stop smoking.*)

The DOCTOR *is writing, with a stylish gold pen,* HARRIET *watches it slide across the paper.*

DOCTOR. Everything nice and normal at home? Not having to rush around too much I hope?

HARRIET (*lightly*). Everything's fine. We have a crazy aunt of Hugh's staying with us, who was shut up in a loony bin for over 60 years, and makes strange smells all over the house (*the* DOCTOR *not looking up, not reacting*) and she lies awake every night banging a tin plate against a radiator while making a whining noise, otherwise everything's perfectly normal.

DOCTOR (*not looking up*). Relatives tend to come in all shapes and sizes don't they? Turn up at awkward moments, too, always happening. (*The* DOCTOR *looks up.*) And how has your husband greeted this happy news? The baby coming? Is he as pleased as he should be?

HARRIET. He doesn't know.

DOCTOR (*startled, for the first time letting his cool be ruffled*). He doesn't know! Why?

HARRIET (*ironic laugh*). He doesn't need to know, does he?

Interior: London House: Hall – Day

HARRIET *comes through the door into the hall, to be greeted by a strange sight. The house is absolutely full of flowers, large bouquets and bunches of freshly cut flowers.* HARRIET *moves through the hall in surprise.* LILLIAN *is sitting among the flowers on the half landing, staring out of the window. On one of the bouquets hanging over the bannister is a large greeting card saying 'well done, my darling'.*

HARRIET. What's going on? (*To* LILLIAN.) What's all this about? Did you see who did this?

LILLIAN. They told me not to touch.

The phone rings. HARRIET, *with her carrier bags, has to squeeze past* LILLIAN *on the half landing, to get to the phone. She answers the phone on the main landing, close enough for* LILLIAN *to be able to hear.*

HARRIET. Yes!

HUGH'S VOICE (*loud, excited*). Am I right? I guessed right, didn't I? It's true, isn't it?

HARRIET (*very sharp*). Guessed what?

HUGH. We're going to have a baby! You've done it, my darling. Haven't you?

HARRIET. How on earth did you know?

Interior: HUGH*'s Office – Day*

We see HUGH *in impressive city office with glass walls onto larger open plan office. The telephone conversation is intercut.*

HUGH. I guessed from the number of times you were going to the doctor.

HARRIET. You guessed from me going to the doctor! Really? I thought you'd been following me for a moment.

HUGH. I don't need to do that!

HARRIET. What if you'd been wrong Hugh, what if I'd got AIDS or something? (HUGH *doesn't seem to hear, she shouts down the phone.*) AIDS!

LILLIAN *staring at her.*

HUGH. Harriet really! Don't make jokes like that, it's not like you! Got to go now. Congratulations my love. (*He whispers.*) Our long wait is over!

HUGH *replaces the receiver in his comfortable glass-fronted office in a merchant bank. He turns, smiling broadly to a young secretary in the room.*

I was right. (*The girl smiles.*) I knew I was, I was right. Come on – get some glasses. (*He goes into the open plan office to tell some more people.*) We're going to celebrate!

Interior: London House: Hall/Landing – Day

Rain flicking down the window, LILLIAN's face in profile, staring benignly out through the rain spattered window, watching the blank wall opposite with interest as if watching a film screen.

HARRIET moving past, dressed to go out, catches her coat on the chair. LILLIAN has positioned her seat directly in the middle of the passage.

HARRIET turns, suddenly surprises herself by being really sharp with LILLIAN.

HARRIET. Do you have to sit there – of all places! It's a big house, you don't have to sit right here, you're in the way of everybody. It's really dumb – putting yourself there.

LILLIAN continues to stare out of the window, not even registering HARRIET's presence. HARRIET stands there rattling her car keys.

What's so interesting down there anyway?

For a second, both of them stare at the blank wall.

HARRIET (*as she stands, staring at the blank wall*). We're having a party apparently – quite a big one, celebrating something or other, and I have to go and do the shopping. Hugh has made a list, surprise, surprise . . . (*She begins to go, then turns.*) You don't want to come, do you? (LILLIAN *very slightly turns.*) You haven't been out since you arrived here – I think you better come. OK? (HARRIET *bends over* LILLIAN *their faces close.*) Was that a nod? Just a tiny hint of a nod? Was it? Can you understand what I'm saying?

LILLIAN stares back out of the window.

HARRIET suddenly takes her by the arm, and begins to lift her out of the chair.

Come on, you're coming anyway.

Exterior: London Streets/Interior: Car

HARRIET driving in HUGH's silver Daimler, LILLIAN trussed up in her seat belt next to her, her head right back in the seat, as if she is riding on a roller-coaster.

The car radio is on one of the pop channels – a guess the mystery voice competition, callers trying to identify the name of some actor.
HARRIET *hunched over the wheel, smoking.*

HARRIET. I should stop smoking for the child, shouldn't I? (*To* LILLIAN.) I should stop.

HARRIET *takes another drag,* LILLIAN *staring ahead, her head pressed back.*

Why you sitting like that? We're not about to break the sound barrier or something. (*Warm smile.*) You look as if you want a crash helmet. (HARRIET *is hardly looking at the road.*) *Don't worry.*

LILLIAN'*s eyes are half shut.*

Don't you want to take a look? Have you really not been out for all those years? I don't believe it. So what do you think of everything, Lillian?

Shots of young girls walking along the streets, kids in groups moving down the pavement, the car is travelling behind a large paper lorry, pieces fluttering out of it towards them. HARRIET *swings the car round a corner rapidly.*

If you really hadn't been out, you'd be overwhelmed by all this wouldn't you? (*Glancing at* LILLIAN.) Things have changed haven't they?

As they round the corner, they are greeted by brewery wagon, drawn by black horses moving at a stately pace down the road, the wagon ridden by liveried men in top hats.

(*Laughs.*) That's just an advertisement, take no notice of that.

LILLIAN *staring at the horses as they over-take, a private, contained look in her eyes.*

HARRIET *putting her foot down, car roaring down the street. She's calling out at the radio mystery voice competition.*

Ronald Colman . . . Errol Flynn . . . It's one of those

Hollywood gents, who do you think it is? Do you recognize it? (*Lightly, glancing at* LILLIAN.) I used to be an actress, you know a sort of part time, very tiny roles kind of actress . . . before I met Hugh. Would you have ever guessed that? (*She laughs.*) Used to play the bitches that get killed off halfway through the first act in Agatha Christie. Type casting, don't you think! (*Sharp laugh.*) I expect I was awful really . . .

HARRIET *brakes violently.* LILLIAN *has taken her safety belt off, and is making a movement, as if she's about to open the door.*

What the hell are you doing?

LILLIAN. I don't think I'm allowed to be here, it's not permitted. I will get into trouble.

HARRIET. You can't get into trouble anymore, relax.

Exterior: Shopping Centre – Day

Outside large concrete shopping complex, in the car park, HARRIET *trying to squeeze the car into a small space.* LILLIAN *standing on the pavement, watching her.*

HARRIET (*shouting out of the window*). Have I got room . . . have I got enough room?

LILLIAN *stands watching, she moves her head slightly.*

(*Shouting.*) Is that a nod?

There is a crunching noise.

(*Sharp laugh.*) Oh to hell with it. (*Gets out, starts to walk away.*) This is Hugh's car, I shouldn't be using it for shopping. I'm not even going to look! Come on.

Interior: Supermarket – Day

HARRIET *and* LILLIAN *moving through a sizeable upmarket supermarket.*

They are both pushing large trolleys in front of them. HARRIET *scrambling around for* HUGH's *list.*

HARRIET. Hugh's lists are always so beautifully planned, they
follow the layout of the shop exactly. It says 'start at the cheese
counter . . . and then move in a clockwise direction. . . ' Which
is clockwise? Where's the cheese? (*She goes over.*) Here we go . . .

HARRIET *starts to order at cheese and delicatessen counter. She
doesn't notice that* LILLIAN *has wandered off on her own.*

(*To an empty space.*) I hope you are not going to find this party
too much of an ordeal Lillian . . . I mean all the surviving
family being there.

The shop assistant looks at her oddly.

We cut to LILLIAN *wandering down the aisles of the supermarket,
staring intrigued at all the stacks of goods. She moves closer to a tall
pile of biscuits, being marketed in tins with evocative nostalgic period
pictures on the front, and called 'Old English Biscuit' selection. She
takes several tins and puts them in her trolley. She takes them from
the middle of the pyramid display of tins, and moves off, leaving it
standing incredibly perilously balanced on one tin.*

LILLIAN *picks up large 'Special Offer' signs, plucking them off the
rows of food and cans and 'New Range' of pre-cooked meals, and
drops the signs into her trolley, until she has quite a pile of them,
wheeling them along the aisles as if about to purchase them. People
are eyeing her oddly, but* LILLIAN *is moving on, oblivious, pushing
her trolley.*

*She stops at the frozen meat counter, and surveys a display of frozen
joints of beef, lamb and whole ducks. She picks up a frozen duck
from the fridge, then another, then another. We cut back to*
HARRIET *still ordering from* HUGH's *list, totally immersed in it.*

We cut back to LILLIAN, *she has about eight or nine frozen ducks
now in her trolley, she has put a couple of biscuit tins in the fridge,
to make room for them. She also drops most of the pile of 'Special
Offer' signs into the fridge, leaving only two small signs in among the
ducks.*

*People are standing watching her, out of the corner of their eyes,
having stopped their own shopping.*

We cut to LILLIAN *waiting patiently in the check-out queue, a benign innocent look on her face, with her great pile of frozen meat in her trolley.*

LILLIAN *gets to the cashier, it is her turn.*

CASHIER (*lifting the 'Special Offer' signs out from amongst the frozen ducks*). You don't want these I don't think, do you? Must've fallen in somehow. But you'll need the trolley I expect.

LILLIAN *watches intrigued as the total is rattled up on the cash register, a second assistant helpfully puts the meat in bags and puts them back in the trolley.*

LILLIAN *smiles at them, a slight, peaceful smile. The receipt is snaking its way out of the machine.*

That'll be £122.53 pence please love.

LILLIAN *nods sweetly at them and, without making any move to pay, pushes her trolley straight on through the check out and towards the automatic glass doors, that hiss open, as she approaches with the vast pile of frozen meat.*

Immediate alarms go off, and assistant and shop managers converge from all corners of the shop and surround LILLIAN.

We cut to HARRIET's *head spinning round, in her part of the shop.*

HARRIET. Lillian?

HARRIET *runs across the shop, shouting 'wait, wait, she's with me, don't do anything, she's with me'.*

She passes the pyramid of biscuits, that collapses as she runs past scattering across the aisle.

She reaches the group, just as they're escorting LILLIAN *towards an office.*

Exterior: Shopping Centre – Day

Cut to LILLIAN *sitting on a bench outside, totally impervious, sitting watching the cars.*

Interior: Supermarket – Day

We cut inside the shop, HARRIET *is standing surrounded by assistants, and the trolley of frozen meat. A little man is remonstrating, jabbing his finger at* HARRIET. *She is bright red with fury, and is waving a frozen duck round in her hand.*

HARRIET (*shouting*). Why do I have to buy it? I'll put it back! If you let me for chrissake. The meat's begun to defrost? That's rubbish! That's because we've been standing here for twenty minutes, you idiots! (*She grabs a biscuit tin, waving it furiously.*) The bloody biscuits haven't begun to defrost, have they?

Exterior: Shopping Centre – Day

We cut back to LILLIAN *sitting blissfully on her seat. She is watching some kids weaving their way through the cars, trying the door handles of the parked cars. They get to the Daimler, try the door, and then break the back side window with expert ease. One of them looks up at* LILLIAN *just as he is reaching in to unlock the door.* LILLIAN *continues to watch, even gives them a little smile. The kid smiles back, and gets inside to steal the radio.*

HARRIET *comes out of the shop wheeling the frozen ducks, just as the kids scamper away from the car.* HARRIET *sees them go with the radio.*

HARRIET. I don't believe it. I just don't believe it! (*To* LILLIAN, *furiously.*) Why didn't you tell me, you idiot! You just watched, did you! (*She begins to run towards the car.*) Hugh will kill me. (*She turns in the car park and yells back at* LILLIAN.) This is the last time we ever go shopping you hear! (*Really loud.*) You understand!

Exterior: London House – Day

LILLIAN *by window, overlooking the street, staring down as Bentleys, taxis, one or two BMWs and Porsches are rolling up into the short drive in front of the house.*

People getting out, dressed smartly for a party, a chauffeur being told when to come and pick up a couple of guests. LILLIAN *looking tense as she watches them all arrive.*

Interior: Drawing room – Day

Cut to subjective shot, LILLIAN'*s point of view, the door opening into the main reception rooms. A large buffet party is in full swing – a magnificent spread of food, dominated by all the duck* LILLIAN *bought.*

There is a range of people present, spreading from HUGH'*s relatives to some of* HARRIET'*s friends, a couple of people that could have been actors with her. But mostly it is* LILLIAN'*s surviving family, the relations, old ladies, elderly stout men with jowelly faces, and their offspring. The room is ringing with small talk and the sound of eating, people are also spilling into the ample garden.*

DOMINIC *is standing staring carefully at the guests, dressed in smart little suit, he surveys everything with a cool stare, sucking a drink through a straw. He moves up to two city friends of* HUGH, *still sucking out of the straw.*

MAN (*patronising smile*). Hello Dominic, we were just . . .

DOMINIC. Talking about house prices. Yes I heard. Please carry on, it's one of my best subjects.

Nobody seems to notice LILLIAN *for a moment. She stands on the edge of the room, for a moment watching them all, her old family, spread out before her.*

She sees two old ladies talking in a corner, looking in her direction, and exchanging knowing looks.

HARRIET *suddenly appears by* LILLIAN'*s side, she is strikingly dressed and in a febrile, extrovert mood.*

HARRIET. You're going to eat something aren't you Lillian? (*She smiles.*) You see all the ducks here! (*She turns to one of the guests.*) The food is largely Lillian's contribution . . . she chose most of it.

LILLIAN *is watching her.*

You must drink Lillian. (*Pouring her some champagne.*)
Celebrate, and really enjoy yourself, there are lots of people
here who want to meet you, they're already queuing up.

LILLIAN *flinches away.*

*The two old women she saw gossiping about her in the corner, bear
down on her.*

One of them pushes her face right up to LILLIAN, *as if addressing
a very deaf child.*

MATILDA. You don't remember me, I'm sure. I am Matilda . . .
do you remember? You came to stay with me in Horsham, one
summer holiday, when *I* was a girl.

MATILDA *looks older than* LILLIAN.

And we quarrelled the whole time.

The other woman, GLADYS, *sharp faced and smaller, pushes in.*

GLADYS (*to* MATILDA). She doesn't remember. She can't
remember, don't you understand? (*She moves* MATILDA *away
for a moment whispering loudly.*) She isn't even able to remember
who she is. Poor dear . . . you can't ask her questions, there's
no point, she's just like a gentle vegetable, shut up all that time
. . . in that building.

GLADYS *then returns, to talk to* LILLIAN *herself, she speaks
slowly, too, and for some reason feels she has better chance of
making herself understood, if she traces the shapes of the words in the
air.*

I came to visit you once . . . and you look just the same *now* as
you did then (*She smiles.*) Isn't that nice? (GLADYS *moves off.*)
Must just get myself some of that duck pâté.

LILLIAN *begins to move away, but suddenly* MATILDA *appears
again, pushing her face towards her.*

MATILDA. Must find somewhere to sit down.

MATILDA *looks at* LILLIAN *as if she expects* her *to find a
chair.* LILLIAN *does not move.*

No, don't you do anything, I'm sure I can manage myself, I've not been too well recently, had to keep on going to see the doctor.

LILLIAN (*looking straight at her*). Why? Is it because you've got AIDS?

MATILDA *looks astonished.*

If you've been going to the doctor a lot, it could be AIDS.

LILLIAN *begins to move off.*

MATILDA (*calling after her*). Whatever they've been trying to do to you in that place Lillian, it certainly hasn't worked.

We cut to LILLIAN *in another corner of the room. She stands watching two fleshy-faced, plump elderly men who look like brothers, one only slightly older than the other, in conversation with a rather elegant woman who is nodding vigorously.*

We track in on the jowelly faces of the two men, then back onto LILLIAN'*s eyes. One of the men has noticed her watching, and instinctively, turns away. Like they have been talking about her. The other brother then glances in her direction, uneasy under her stare, and then looks away. The noise of the party getting louder.*

We're back on LILLIAN'*s face, sudden churning flashbacks begin, like a stream of thought inside her has suddenly been uncorked. Rapid glimpses, piling vividly on top of each other.*

Flashback: Interior London House – Drawing Room – Day

We see a young, vital, slightly wild looking girl of about fifteen, a sense of trapped energy, in contrast to the plush upholstered worlds we see her passing through.

We see her face in close up watching through a crack in the door, staring into a large drawing room in the twenties, watching her family at a formal tea party with guests. A subjective shot of her entering the room, her clothes and hair are wet, her legs bare, people looking at her, very disquietened by her entrance.

We see she is holding a dead hedgehog, she lifts the silver cake cover up and places the hedgehog next to a walnut cake. Then she walks across and sits down.

YOUNG LILLIAN (*watching the startled guests*). Somebody trod on it in the garden. I thought you'd like to see it.

We see LILLIAN's *spiky faced sister* MARGARET *watching her, appalled.*

Flashback: Interior: London House – Day

We cut to another plush interior and see YOUNG LILLIAN *jumping up and down on an ornamental sofa, a powerful unstoppable, surge of energy as she sings, almost chanting rhythmically, a song of the period again and again, getting faster with each jump. Till she's leaping like on a trampoline.*

Flashback: Exterior: Alleyway – Day

We then see her in an alleyway with two boys that look like brothers, one slightly older than the other. They are standing in the rain, the older boy tells the younger one to get lost. And then the remaining brother and the YOUNG LILLIAN *are passionately kissing. Slipping down in between a crack in the wall, and water streams from gutters round them, and people watch from a window opposite, but they are oblivious, rolling in the mud and the water.*

COUSIN EDWARD (*laughing, close to her face*). You do it so well, Lillian!

YOUNG LILLIAN's *face in profile, water dripping off her.*

YOUNG LILLIAN. You think so? (*She kisses him passionately.*) I have been practising – just for you. . . (*Another sensual, experienced kiss.*) . . . only for you.

Flashback: Interior: Drawing Room – Day

We cut to the YOUNG LILLIAN *watching a recital, a concert in the drawing room, a relative or member of the family is intoning a poem of his own composition, with suitable music on a gramophone behind him, creating the right ambience. But* YOUNG LILLIAN *is suddenly laughing in the hushed atmosphere, at the reverential delivery and the solemn music behind, a loud spontaneous laugh. Each time he does another line, she laughs louder, she gets off her chair, onto the floor repeating the last line he's just recited and dissolving into shrieks of laughter.*

Flashback: Interior: Drawing Room – Night

We cut to a large room after a party, covered in paper streamers, and crushed party hats and food, YOUNG LILLIAN *screaming and shouting as the brother we saw her kissing walks past her. He is getting his hat and coat, she tears his scarf away as he passes her and then starts breaking glasses, throwing them in several directions at once, like a catherine wheel going off, as she implores him not to leave.*

Flashback: Interior: YOUNG LILLIAN's *Room – Night*

We cut to her father coming into her room, her own little room, with the curtains drawn, a dark private space, where the walls are covered in weird pictures of distorted faces, forming strange patterns across the wall. Her father, a straight, comfortable looking man, stares at her and then at the faces on the wall. Among the faces is one very obviously of him, looking grotesque and comic.

The same picture HARRIET *saw on the wall of the mental hospital when she was waiting in the passage.*

FATHER (*staring down at her*). What on earth are you doing in here Lillian?

YOUNG LILLIAN (*looking up, staring directly at him*). Nothing. Enjoying myself. (*She stares at the grotesque picture on the wall.*) Reminding myself what you really look like.

Flashback: Interior: Drawing Room – Day

Then we cut to the two brothers entering a room and walking past her, towards a row of seats where a formal group photograph of the entire family is about to be taken. There are thirty individuals present, all dressed up. The older brother passes YOUNG LILLIAN *and fails to respond to her calling his name. As he moves to try to take his seat, he is caught by the* YOUNG LILLIAN, *holding onto his leg, and she won't let go. As he moves away she continues to hold onto him, and as he walks across the room, he drags her along the floor behind him for a few paces, incredibly embarrassed, as the whole family looks on.*

Her sister MARGARET *is looking particularly stunned and appalled.*

YOUNG LILLIAN (*calling out passionately as she holds onto him*).
Look at me, PLEASE. Just look at me. (*Yelling from the heart.*)
Why are you doing this to me? I'm not going to go away. I'M
GOING TO MAKE YOU LOOK AT ME!

The Party: Main Drawing Room: The Present

We cut back to the party, and the present, and the fleshy faces of the two men, the two brothers as they are now, one of them is shovelling a piece of celery into a cheese dip, gulping it up, and talking vigorously at the same time, how he 'always knew the hovercraft would never be much of a success . . . how he'd told everyone, but nobody had listened'.

LILLIAN *watches the two brothers.*

LILLIAN (*to nobody in particular*). I think it was the older one
. . . I'm not sure . . . (*Louder.*) I can't remember which was the
one I liked. I don't remember! (*Slight smile.*) Can't tell them
apart now, anyway.

The sharp faced old woman, GLADYS, *is passing at this moment, half overhears.*

GLADYS. What dear? You don't know which is your glass? (*As if to a child.*) Just take another, that's what we do at a party like this. (GLADYS *starts pouring her another glass.*) You're allowed to drink all this are you?

LILLIAN *turns, watching the champagne fill the glass – a sudden swift flashback as if her thoughts have started again.*

Flashback: Interior: London House, Nursery – Day

A high shot of YOUNG LILLIAN, *lying as if after sex with the elder brother, on a carpet somewhere, surrounded by toys, like they are in* LILLIAN's *old nursery. Both of them are laughing, and she's kicking in a lazy, sensual way at an old rocking horse in front of them.*

YOUNG LILLIAN (*her spontaneous laugh*). They think this is where I belong still. (*She looks serious for a moment, an intense stare.*) Nobody knows what to do with me . . . (*She begins to draw idly, sensually with a piece of charcoal on his bare back.*) Don't move, don't move . . .

The image begins to cloud, as if this is where she's beginning to lose the clarity of her thoughts . . . the image burning out to white, as HUGH's *voice cuts in and we land back at the party with a jolt.*

The Present: Interior: Drawing Room – Day

HUGH (*smiling*). Can I have your attention please. (*Mock authoritarian.*) ATTENTION PLEASE, there at the back.

HUGH *standing on a chair, surveying the family gathering, contented faces, now just beginning to get drunk.*

We're here on this happy occasion – for three reasons.

Calls from some of those watching 'only three' 'Hugh you're slipping' etc.

Apart from seeing all of you of course (*loud*) the *first* reason – this is Harriet and mine, this is our tenth wedding anniversary. This very day.

Applause, calls of 'fifty more to go', 'is it only ten years, seems much longer' etc.

Second – to welcome my Aunt Lillian back – her return from (*he stops*) a long time away (*with feeling*) an unnecessarily long time – to put it mildly.

A ripple of 'Hear hears', people not quite certain how to react, looking at their feet embarrassed; one or two people glance in her direction and give little nods, and half-toasts with their glasses. But

LILLIAN *has her back to all of them, seemingly oblivious, eating a piece of duck.*

And thirdly (*he smiles*) we mustn't forget thirdly (*he touches* HARRIET) because there's a little bulge down here. Yes, we're having another baby. (*Smiles.*) At last –

Applause and some drunken Ahs!

HARRIET (*slightly drunk smile*). No need to start telling them how often we've been trying.

HUGH (*lifts glass*). Well we've made it.

As long as I don't let Harriet go out in my car anymore – you should see what Lillian and she managed to do to it!

Cut to HUGH *blowing out candles on a cake marked 'H and H – the first ten years'.* HARRIET *is brandishing a large knife, miming slicing off* HUGH's *head as he blows the candle, people clapping and laughing.*

Interior: Basement Room – Evening

We cut to much later in the party, evening in the basement room, HARRIET *and* HUGH, *some of her friends and one or two of the elderly relations are playing charades.*

HARRIET *is acting out the film title 'Splendour in the Grass' gesticulating, acting smoking dope, writhing in the grass etc. Her mimes are full of vitality, and quite original. People are calling out 'Venom', 'The Snake Pit', 'Jaws III'. One of the elderly relatives pipes up with 'Dr Zhivago'. There is a pebble-glassed,* MOVIE BUFF *type crouching in the corner, quietly calling out fairly obscure movie titles.*

MOVIE BUFF. Closely Observed Trains. (*As* HARRIET *writhes on the floor.*) The Cow – it's an Iranian movie you know. (*Slowly intoning.*) Woman of the Dunes.

HUGH *is enthusiastically belting out film titles and clapping loudly at each of* HARRIET's *moves. His eyes are shining full of pride at* HARRIET's *acting. He is also holding a stop watch, and calling out every ten seconds how long they've got to get it.*

DOMINIC *is watching his mother objectively, like watching a stranger.*

LILLIAN *is sitting on a high-backed chair in the middle of the room, watching them all.* MATILDA *and* GLADYS, *having drunk rather a lot, are sitting on the floor a little way away,* GLADYS *has kicked off her shoes.* LILLIAN *overhears them.*

MATILDA. She seems very peaceful doesn't she . . . almost happy I think . . . you wouldn't know anything just looking at her would you . . . And to think of the things she did.

GLADYS. I always used to say she's got a skin missing . . . a whole skin wasn't there – she felt everything so *extremely.*

MATILDA. Part of her brain missing I would say. Its marvellous how Hugh and Harriet treat her so normally.

HARRIET *has stopped – somebody has at last guessed the title.*

As HARRIET *moves to take her seat,* HUGH *catches her by the wrist.*

HUGH. That was good, the Hippy you did, that was especially funny.

HARRIET (*embarrassed in front of her friends*). Yes, OK darling, alright.

She pulls away, but HUGH *hasn't finished.*

HUGH. No, no, the dope smoking and everything was really effective, really gruesome. (*To somebody sitting next to him.*) It was almost up to professional standard, wasn't it. Yes I thought so . . . (*He smiles.*) She hasn't forgotten it all yet, acting. (*Knowing tone.*) Far from it, I can tell you, when she really wants something. (*Very warm smile at* HARRIET *who has sat down by now.*) Well done darling.

HARRIET *stares back at him across the room. She catches* LILLIAN's *eye, watching her closely. The* MOVIE BUFF *who is very drunk says without thinking.*

MOVIE BUFF. Why doesn't Lillian have a go? It's Lillian's turn now?

HUGH (*embarrassed, jumps up immediately*). No – I think we've had enough now. The game's over. Let's see who's left upstairs, see what they are getting up to.

As HUGH *and some of the other guests begin to leave the room,* LILLIAN *suddenly starts singing . . . in a quiet hoarse voice, an obscure song of her childhood, that is a little difficult to make out, but quite tuneful.*

HARRIET, HUGH *and the others all stop at the door, watching this. It doesn't last long.* LILLIAN *stops in mid verse and stares back at them.*

HUGH (*with feeling*). That was very nice Lillian . . . excellent.

HARRIET *is staring straight at* LILLIAN *with a shrewd look.*

Interior: Basement Room – Night

Cut to the empty downstairs room, drinks, party hats, streamers, squashed food all over the floor.

HARRIET, *rather drunk, is crouching on her hands and knees on the floor, tidying up.* LILLIAN *still sitting in the same chair.*

HARRIET. Aren't people pigs! . . . look at this mess. (HARRIET *surrounded by the remains of the party.*)

HUGH *enters, picking his way gingerly over the mess.*

HUGH. You haven't got very far, have you? (*He looks at the smashed food, the half eaten plates of leftovers.*) Maybe we can use some of this again – must try to salvage some of it. Be pity to waste it all.

He begins to move to go, LILLIAN *and* HARRIET *watching him; he turns.*

You haven't been smoking again Harriet?

HARRIET. Hardly.

HUGH *picks up fag ends that she has left in a line, standing on their ends on the mantlepiece.*

HUGH. Are these yours? This looks like you.

He pulls a plastic bag out of his pocket, a see-through plastic bag and starts dropping the fag ends into it, one by one.

You *know* its stupid, but you still go ahead and do it. (*Sorrowful tone.*) Amazing obstinacy. (*Dropping the last one into the bag.*) I'm going to keep these as a reminder, hang them up in the bedroom (*closing bag*) – no, I am. Now hurry up, its extremely late, you don't want to be up too late darling, do you?

He leaves.

HARRIET. What are you looking like that for? (*She stops.*) Aren't you going to help?

LILLIAN *staring at her.*

Sorry – I didn't mean that. (*Loud.*) Yes – maybe I *did* mean that. (*She moves up to* LILLIAN *on all fours.*) Because you don't fool me – do you Lillian? You haven't fooled me – from the start.

LILLIAN *impassive,* HARRIET *crouching by her on the chair, their faces very close.*

Because you know far more about what's going on than you pretend – don't you. You understand *everything* don't you but you're refusing to show it. (*Drunken smile.*) You prefer to seem an idiot . . .

LILLIAN *giving her nothing, staring straight back at her eyes.*

I know you don't like me – but I want you to know. (HARRIET *puts her hands on either side of* LILLIAN's *face.*) I've seen through you – do you understand my dear . . . maybe you're having a little laugh at me right at this moment.

HARRIET *and* LILLIAN's *faces together in close up.*

You're a fraud Lillian – quite a good one, but a fraud. Aren't you? Give a little nod, go *on.*

LILLIAN's *head remains completely still. A direct completely neutral stare straight back at* HARRIET.

It's OK, I don't mind, nobody else need ever know.

Interior: The Dining Room – Day

We cut to HARRIET, *tottering down to breakfast in her dressing gown.*

DOMINIC *is sitting at the table eating two fried eggs on fried bread.* HARRIET's *stomach practically turns over on seeing this. She sits looking fragile, rather beautiful, her face very pale, sipping her coffee, and watching huge dripping mouthfuls go into her son's mouth.* LOUISE *is there too.*

DOMINIC. You look terrible mummy, you look like you are going to be sick any minute. (*Putting another mouthful in.*) Are you going to be sick any minute?

HARRIET. Dominic please . . . (*Glancing over at* DOMINIC.) How did I produce such a crude specimen? Where did you come from? I don't know . . .

THERESA *coming in with another plate of eggs.*

Not more. Don't have some more please. Theresa take it away.

DOMINIC (*firmly*). Theresa put it down. (THERESA *hesitates.*) At once.

THERESA *puts it down hastily and moves to start cleaning in the background.*

HARRIET (*watching this*). Nobody listens to me in this house at all!

DOMINIC (*with egg*). It's great. (*He starts eating, with relish.*) You are always cross with me – do you know that, mummy? I've been counting – its 160 days since you last said something nice.

HARRIET. Is that all? (*She smiles.*) I had no idea we were getting on so well lately.

DOMINIC. It's at least 200 days since you said something nice – and *meant* it. (*Another mouthful of egg.*) I bet you've been counting the days till I go back to school. (*He glances up.*)

HARRIET. That's right – I cross them off each day. (*Lightly.*) It's a huge relief when the end's in sight.

DOMINIC (*busying himself with his plate*). For me too . . .

HARRIET. Don't be silly darling. (*Her voice matter-of-fact.*) I hate it when you go back. You know that.

DOMINIC *not looking at her.*

(*Suddenly her head turning*). Where is the smell? (*To* LOUISE.) The horrible fishy smell Lillian is always making at this time – where is it?

LOUISE. Oh Mrs Ambrose – Lillian went.

HARRIET (*startled*). What do you mean, went?

LOUISE (*very agitated now*). She said she had to do it, she had to go. She had to leave.

DOMINIC (*eating a piece of toast now*). Oh yes, she went about 10 minutes ago – didn't I tell you? I meant to – she just walked out of the house. Didn't even say goodbye. (*Bites into toast.*) Can't blame her really.

HARRIET (*jumping up*). She can't go out on her own. DON'T YOU SEE! That's the one thing we were told about! . . . She can't even cross the road . . . ! (*Really alarmed,* HARRIET *moves backwards and forwards, by the table.*)

Theresa – ring Mr Ambrose, tell him what's happened – tell him to get back here *now*. (*Shouts.*) Right *now*, don't accept any excuses, get him here now!

HARRIET *opens the door and runs out into the street in her dressing gown.*

Exterior: London House – Day

HARRIET *stands for a moment on the pavement, shouting back at* DOMINIC *and* LOUISE *watching her from the front door,* HARRIET*'s dressing gown and nightdress blowing about.*

HARRIET. She can't have got far! I'm just . . .

Exterior: London Street – Day

HARRIET *runs down the street, she turns the corner into the main road.*

There is a row of shops on the corner and an office of a design consultancy with several men sitting at desks in front of the tinted glass window which is at street level.

HARRIET *runs into the office in her dressing gown. Two of the men look up at her very startled.*

HARRIET. Did you see an old lady pass by just now? (*They look blank.*) An old lady . . . on her own? About this high? Looking lost, looking like she'd never seen a car before – DID YOU SEE HER? (*She's furious, looking at them.*) Jesus, what you all staring at? Nobody see her? She must have come by here? . . .

MAN AT DESK. If we see her. . . ?

HARRIET. Call the police if you see her! Is that simple enough for you to understand? And all of you watch, watch OK – she may come back this way!

HARRIET *goes out into the street. Glancing around anxiously. Wherever she looks, she sees old ladies. Sitting on a bench, standing at a zebra crossing, walking along slowly in front of the shops.*

HARRIET *goes up to a bus queue, who watch her approach with some amusement.*

Did you see an old lady pass by here . . . ? (*They stare at her,* HARRIET *looks rather wild in her dressing gown.*) She would have looked like she was completely lost – in a daze, wandering about? (*Really angry as she sees somebody smirking.*) Don't laugh – just answer a perfectly simple question, did you see somebody? (*Blank faces staring at her.*) Jesus, what a wretched collection of people.

Thanks very much.

HARRIET *turns, runs along the street a little way.*

This is ridiculous, I'm never going to find her like this.

HARRIET *sees a male* TRAFFIC WARDEN *standing there.* HARRIET *grabs him by the arm.*

You've been keeping an eye out no doubt – have you seen an old lady?

WARDEN. An old lady? No, I'm only looking at vehicles I'm afraid.

HARRIET (*very sharp*). Great! (*She looks about the street, heavy lorries on the road, she's suddenly really worried.*) How am I going to find her for Chrissake!

Exterior: London Roads/Interior: Car – Day

HARRIET *driving in* HUGH's *car, the Daimler, driving fast. She dressed so quickly she's still straightening the sweater she's wearing as she drives, she's also talking into the car phone at the same time, waving the phone about. We intercut with* HUGH, *in his glass office.*

HARRIET. Hugh – have you got through to the home yet? (*Loud.*) You know the *HOME*! The hospital, whatever you call it . . .

HUGH. There's no answer, I've tried several times.

HARRIET *driving erratically with one hand – sometimes no hands.*

HARRIET. We've got to get their help, they'll know what to do . . . I'm going to go there.

She puts her foot down in the car.

HUGH. Going there! Don't be stupid darling.

HARRIET. Be quicker than waiting for you to get through! And what about the police?

HUGH (*patient tone*). I don't want to bring them into it yet, darling.

HARRIET. Why not for chrissake!

HUGH. This is something we can do. We don't want Aunt Lillian involved with the police, there might be publicity.

HARRIET. Publicity! Who the hell's interested in Lillian – or the family for that matter?

HUGH (*firmly*). She's only gone for a walk Harriet – that's all that's happened – I'm going now to look in Holland Park, because that's where she'll be. That's where I told you to look.

HARRIET *driving faster and faster.*

HUGH's *voice.* I don't know why you haven't looked there. She's not capable of going any further . . . And take care of the *car* won't you.

Exterior: Drive of Mental Hospital – Day

High shot above the drive of the mental hospital, as HARRIET *roars through the gates and up the drive, bouncing on the uncertain surface of the cracked, ill-kept drive.*

She brakes fiercely as the car heads directly towards the skip and the builders, she practically knocks one of them over as the car pulls up.

HARRIET *leaps out and runs through the clouds of builders' dust, even thicker now than it was, into the building.*

Interior: Mental Hospital – Day

HARRIET *runs through the main entrance, at the reception there is an elderly woman watching an old black and white TV. She looks totally blank when* HARRIET *calls out to her.*

HARRIET. Is Lillian here? Lillian Huckle. Has she come back? I thought she *might* have come back.

ELDERLY WOMAN. I don't deal with the patients.

Interior: Mental Hospital, Corridor and Ward – Day

HARRIET *runs down the passage which is deserted, she smashes through the makeshift barrier sending bits of it scattering all over the place. She runs past the green fish tanks, and turns into the ward, which has now only one bed left in it, and a chair by the window.*

On the chair, LILLIAN *is sitting, staring out of her usual window.*

HARRIET *(shouts with relief). Thank God* you're here, Lillian.

LILLIAN *with her back to* HARRIET. LILLIAN's *head moves, but she doesn't turn round.*

We were so worried . . .

HARRIET's *relief turns quickly to fury, as* LILLIAN *hardly acknowledges her presence.*

Don't you ever, *ever* do this again. Leave without telling anybody. DO YOU HEAR?

HARRIET *moves up to* LILLIAN *really shouting.*

Do you hear me? (*Loud.*) We didn't know what had happened to you!

LILLIAN. What's going on? I don't know why you're shouting.

LILLIAN *turns her head, leans round in her chair.*

Why is she shouting? Do you know?

HARRIET *suddenly sees they are not alone, three old people, two old men and a woman are sitting on the one remaining bed in a corner. All with coats on, like they have travelled back too. One of them is* GEORGE, *the old man we saw in the ballroom at the beginning of the film.*

HARRIET (*staring at them*). They came back as well did they? (*Quiet.*) None of you can keep away . . .

She stares at them.

The NURSE *comes into the ward.*

NURSE (*as she enters*). No – they've been drifting back over the last few days, as soon as we get one to leave, another one tries to come back. (*Looks at* HARRIET *sharply.*) Glad you have come for her anyway. If they all had somebody it would be easier. Now Lillian – you *know* you shouldn't be here.

LILLIAN *absolutely still, not going to move.*

Interior: Ballroom – Day

Cut to HARRIET *and the* NURSE *trying to coax* LILLIAN *through the door of the ballroom, and across the room towards the main entrance, but* LILLIAN *is holding on tightly to the side of the door, calm expression, but very determined. She doesn't want to be moved.*

NURSE. She'll come . . . don't worry . . . Just a little reluctant, but she'll come. Won't you Lillian . . . Just let go, come on love.

HARRIET (*pleading*). Please, Lillian, you can't stay here, the ward's closed, they've closed *your* ward, its gone. I know you can understand that. (*To* NURSE.) I'm sure she can understand a lot more than we realize. . .

NURSE. Well we can't have her back, whatever happens. (*Loud.*) Do you hear that Lillian? (*Sharp.*) We don't want to have to use force. . .

LILLIAN *calm but still holding onto the wall tightly. They could easily overpower her, but they are trying to coax her instead, gently taking hold of her arm, then letting go.*

LILLIAN (*simply*). This is the place I want to be.

HARRIET. I'm sorry about what happened last night – I didn't mean it, OK. Is that what you want to hear?

LILLIAN *looking away.*

Is this what this is about? I was drunk, I was really pissed, and I'm saying I'm sorry, OK!

NURSE *watching this, rather intrigued.*

(*To* NURSE.) How did she get here anyway?

NURSE. By taxi.

HARRIET (*pleased smile*). By taxi. I knew you could get around if you wanted. How did she know the address? Does she know where this place is? (*She smiles at* LILLIAN *warmly, her face close.*) I would love to have overheard you giving directions to the cabbie. . .

The NURSE *unclasps* LILLIAN'*s hand.* LILLIAN *is grasping tightly one of the labels from her suitcases, with her name and the address of the hospital on it. The label looks extremely old.*

(*Approvingly.*) That's clever.

LILLIAN *gives her a sharp suspicious look, as if saying 'are you trying to get round me this way'.*

NURSE. She didn't pay though – we had to. (*Handing* HARRIET *the bill.*) It was over seventy pounds.

HARRIET *sees* GEORGE, *the old man, lurking in the shadows, in the doorway behind them.*

HARRIET. I'll take your friend too. We'll give him a lift home. (*Sudden smile at both of them.*) I'll take you both out to tea if you like.

Interior: Fortnums – Afternoon

LILLIAN, GEORGE *and* HARRIET *eating ice-creams at Fortnums or similar luxury tea rooms.* LILLIAN *and* GEORGE *tucking into their large ice-creams.* HARRIET *watching them closely, just dipping into hers with small spoonfuls.*

GEORGE *is talking at the top of his voice, a stream of things, jumping in the middle of sentences making only partial sense. His voice switching from matter-of-fact to real intensity and back.*

People staring from other tables, at some of the things he is saying and at his erratic behaviour, blobs of ice-cream fly around, as he waves his spoon about. But HARRIET *finds herself strangely unembarrassed.*

GEORGE. I escaped twice – I did – under the river, there's a pipe, I knew it was there, I had known about it for a long time. They use it for all sorts of things, my God, if people knew what went on there, who I'd seen going through that pipe. Faces you'd know, oh yes! Household names. Before I used it, I'd seen them from the window, going down to the river. I kept on trying to get away from that, but they were always watching me. (*He turns to* LILLIAN, *suddenly much more coherent.*) I used to get the pillow, the punishment they gave us – I said I'll tell the prime minister what you're doing here, I'll tell Winston Churchill, he was prime minister then, they said go ahead, I wrote about twenty-five letters.

LILLIAN. I remember the letters. They didn't work.

GEORGE (*his voice rising*). They never posted them – because they thought I was dangerous. (*He smiles.*)

Faces turning from their tea and cakes.

(*Loud.*) You know what they did with the pillow, they held it, the held it over your mouth till you were purple, till you could hardly breathe, you were kicking, you were fighting, you were tearing with your hands, but they kept on holding it right there. (*To* LILLIAN.) We both got it, didn't we?

LILLIAN (*eating ice-cream with great poise*). They used to sit on me, two or three of them used to sit on me . . . when I got the pillow.

GEORGE (*suddenly to* HARRIET). And I'll tell you the really interesting thing – they were terribly *bad* at everything they did. They couldn't even do *that* properly. Amateurs . . . (*Bangs table.*) They were hopeless.

LILLIAN. Don't shout like that, eat your ice-cream.

LILLIAN *has authority over* GEORGE.

GEORGE. Don't shout, don't shout, don't shout, don't shout . . . etc.

HARRIET. If you could keep your voice down just a little.

GEORGE. After the pillow . . . (*Chants.*) Get it in the morning, get it in the evening, get it, get it, get it, get it . . . etc.

A rhythmic chant, oblivious to the noise he is making. LILLIAN *joins in with him staring at* HARRIET. *Both of them trying to unsettle* HARRIET. HARRIET *deeply embarrassed for a moment, but then stares directly back at* LILLIAN.

LILLIAN (*to* GEORGE). Eat your ice-cream.

HARRIET. Thank you, that was almost as good as Lillian's song at the party. Do you know any more?

GEORGE (*looking at* HARRIET). You are having a baby?

HARRIET. How did you know that?

She looks at LILLIAN. LILLIAN *pointedly looks away.*

She told you, did she? She won't talk to me . . . but she'll talk to other people.

LILLIAN *not looking up.*

Been gossiping about me, have you?

Exterior: Outside seedy Bed and Breakfast – Afternoon

HARRIET *and* LILLIAN *inside the Daimler, watching* GEORGE *walk up the steps of a really seedy Bed and Breakfast hotel in some back street behind Paddington. Peeling paint, and feel of decay and filth from the building; one of the windows is boarded up with hardboard.*

HARRIET. Does he really have to stay here?

LILLIAN *watching him go.*

It's an even worse dump than that home you're so fond of. (GEORGE *turning to wave.*) Will he be alright? (LILLIAN *glances at her.*) I can only deal with one of you Lillian, OK! Is that a terrible thing to say? No, – anyway it's true.

GEORGE *is standing with his plastic bags, waving, and then sticking his stomach out, making himself into the shape of a pregnant woman, and then giving the thumbs up sign. Pushing out his stomach rather grotesquely.*

What on earth is he doing? He's not going on about the baby again is he? Jesus.

HARRIET *watches him with a slight smile.*

He'll get us all arrested doing that.

Receding shot of GEORGE *on hostel steps.*

Interior: Hospital: Baby Scan – Day

Close up of the scan image, the foetus at 16 weeks, moving, HARRIET *lying staring at the image of her baby from the scan, with a slightly detached stare.*

HUGH *and* DOMINIC *are there too, and a young male doctor murmuring in the background.*

HUGH. Amazing sight, isn't it. That image. It's beautiful. (HUGH *smiles gently.*) He looks just like you.

HARRIET (*lying there, staring at it*). How do you know it's a he?

YOUNG DOCTOR. We don't normally specify the sex at this stage – unless we get a very good shot of the . . .

HUGH. Of the relevant area! Naturally.

HUGH *peers closely at the image trying to make its sex out.*

I just can't quite see . . .

DOMINIC (*to doctor*). I can understand you being cautious, I mean if people painted their room for the baby, pink and then it turned out to be a boy, or painted a whole part of the house blue, the nursery and everything and then it was a girl, they might *sue* you mightn't they?

The doctor looks very startled.

If they'd spent a great deal of money on it I mean . . . they might demand compensation. I think you are being quite wise.

HARRIET. Alright Dominic, you can stop handing out legal advice please for once, just be quiet.

HUGH *moves into a corner of the room, starts talking to the doctor in a confidential whisper, but* HARRIET *can just about hear.*

HUGH (*conspiratorial tone*). She is doing everything right is she? I mean the right diet and everything. (*Thrusting a piece of paper at doctor.*) I've brought a list of a typical few days' meals, that she's eating. (*Pointing at paper.*) Just to interpret, the asterisks mark the dishes she's particularly prone to, and the question marks things that might be of concern. I mean my wife can be, how can I put it? (*Calling back.*) Be with you in a moment darling – my wife can be just a tiny bit scatty sometimes, so you should tell *me*, you know, if everything's being done properly.

YOUNG DOCTOR (*having looked at list*). Looks fine . . . excellent . . . no, she's in splendid condition.

HARRIET *staring at them and then the image on the screen.*
HUGH *again looks at the scan.*

HUGH *moving close to* HARRIET, *his face is shining with delight.*

HUGH. Isn't it marvellous?

Suddenly HARRIET *pulls him down towards her holding onto the back of his head – her tone strangely intense.*

HARRIET. I'm so pleased *you're* so happy my love. . .

Shot of the image of the child on the scan, we move close into it.

Interior: Drawing Room – Day

Slow dissolve from the image of the foetus, to HARRIET *much much larger, 6½ months pregnant. She is sitting sweating profusely in a large chair.*

Across the other side of the room is LILLIAN, *sitting in another chair, not looking at her, her back turned towards* HARRIET.

HUGH *and* DOMINIC *playing with a new computer, giggling and laughing together in another corner of the large room.*

HARRIET *from her position staring out of the window can see* THERESA *busy cleaning the Daimler down in the drive.*

HUGH (*calling over from the computer*). Everything alright my love?

HARRIET (*watching* THERESA *cleaning the car*). Everything's thrilling over here . . . Lillian and I are having such an interesting little talk.

LILLIAN's *head twitches slightly, but she remains sitting with her back to* HARRIET, *not looking at her.*

HARRIET *watching* THERESA *clean the Daimler, it is shining brilliantly, she begins to mutter under her breath.*

I mustn't panic . . . I mustn't panic . . . I mustn't panic.

HUGH's *face suddenly appears beside her, his face pressed close,* HARRIET *very startled, not sure if he has overheard or not.*

HUGH. What love?

HARRIET. Nothing . . . just talking nonsense to myself.

HUGH (*watching her closely*). Some kind of list was it darling? (*His face really close to her.*) A list you were making?

HARRIET. That's right.

HUGH (*whispers*). I don't want Lillian to hear this, but Edward
  has died. Cousin Edward . . . Lillian was very close to him a
  long time ago, he and his brother, I'm sure she doesn't
  remember, but just in case, we're going to have to break it
  gently to her.

Exterior: Cemetery – Day

*Cut to the whole family gathered, many of the same faces as at the
party, now all dressed in black standing in a windswept cemetery. They
are arranged in two large clumps near the grave.*

*We see first the one remaining brother, his jowelly face, staring in
dignified plumpness. And then we see* LILLIAN *standing with*
GLADYS *and* MATILDA *and* HARRIET *staring across at him.*
HUGH *is there looking serious, tall and upright amongst his family.*
DOMINIC *is also there, standing still and serious, watching them all.*

HARRIET. It's quite frightening seeing the whole family in black,
  it doesn't really suit them, to put it mildly.

HARRIET *surveying the massed ranks of* HUGH's *family.*

GLADYS. I hate funerals. (*She glances around at the faces of the
  family.*) Who'll be next?

MATILDA. Poor Lillian – look at her . . . she doesn't remember
  him obviously, doesn't realize what's going on at all.

LILLIAN *standing as the funeral service drones on, she has a smile
on her face, which increases until she is positively beaming.*

At the end of the service the surviving brother passes LILLIAN, *and
gives her a little patronizing nod of recognition.* LILLIAN *shows no
sign in return. As he moves just past her,* LILLIAN *announces to
anybody who is listening.*

LILLIAN. I'm very glad that this has happened.

People look astonished.

It's much less confusing now there's only *one* of them left.

GLADYS *turns to* HARRIET.

GLADYS (*rolling her eyes at* LILLIAN*'s behaviour*). Can you help me get away from this dear as quickly as possible. (*She takes* HARRIET*'s arm as they move off down the path.*) Next time we meet will be under much happier circumstances, I hope. (*She gives* HARRIET*'s stomach a little playful tap.*) Don't forget to invite me to see the baby.

HUGH *sweeps up behind them on the path, puts his arm round* GLADYS.

HUGH. Don't worry, Gladys, you will be in the very first batch, one of the very first visitors. Won't she darling? And that's a promise!

Interior: The Bedroom – Night

Cut to bedroom, HARRIET *in nightdress, sitting on the edge of the bed, staring at herself in the full length mirror with a deep intense stare. We move close in on her eyes.*

HUGH *is in the bathroom, washing himself, brushing his teeth, he has a tape playing, the Eurythmics, humming along to them.*

HUGH. I don't know why I feel so good . . . funerals shouldn't make one I know, it's perverse.

Music, HUGH *calling out over the top of it,* HARRIET *staring in the mirror.*

HARRIET *turns her head and stares up at the plastic bag of cigarette ends, hanging from the ceiling, slowly revolving in the light, like some strange piece of decor, the dead cigarettes clearly visible through the plastic. It is suspended over her side of the bed.*

Doesn't Gladys look incredibly young still? Must be over eighty. It's probably because she's never had a worry in her life. (HUGH *looks at himself in the bathroom mirror.*) That doesn't apply to me does it? . . . Would hate it if somewhere somebody was saying exactly the same thing about me. I really don't think its true, it's been bloody in the city this winter. (*He smiles.*) Trench warfare.

HARRIET *has moved slowly across into the bathroom.* HUGH *singing along to the track.*

HARRIET *switches off the music, watching* HUGH *dry his feet.*

HARRIET. You're always so clean, Hugh.

HUGH. Am I?

HARRIET (*very precisely*). You're an above average washer, no question.

HUGH (*with a gentle smile*). Was the music annoying you? I'm sorry love . . . I don't know why I feel so full of energy. It's you that's meant to have a sudden burst of energy when it gets close.

HARRIET. It's not that close yet, not for two months.

HUGH. No. (*Drying himself.*) It's been such a warm winter, maybe that's something to do with it. (HUGH *rubbing his feet vigorously.*) That reminds me – it's a silly time to mention it now – but don't you think we've been over-heating the house? I keep on having to go round switching off radiators. Try to watch out for that darling, OK? (*A big, broad smile straight at her, as he dries himself.*) It's so lovely and mild at the moment!

HARRIET (*watching him in mirror*). There's a woman in our ante-natal class . . . who's suddenly decided she doesn't want the baby.

HUGH. How extraordinary . . . just like that. (HUGH *carefully putting the top back on the toothpaste.*) What did her husband say?

HARRIET. She came home, didn't say anything, started giving him these little cuffs.

HUGH. Cuffs. What you mean cuffs?

HARRIET. Like this.

She starts giving him cuffs, on his face, at first gently, playfully, hardly touching him, but then getting stronger and stronger, glancing blows on his cheek, till she's slapping him.

HUGH (*catches her hands by the wrist, laughing at this horseplay*). OK – OK – I get the *idea*. Always the actress.

HARRIET *doesn't stop for an instant, and* HUGH *has to really hold her tightly by the wrists.*

I *get the idea Harriet.* (*He stares into her eyes.*) Nothing wrong is there?

HARRIET (*straight back at him*). Wrong? What could be wrong?

It's as if HUGH *senses something about her for a moment.*

HUGH. You don't want to see the doctor or anything?

HARRIET (*sharp*). No.

HUGH. Fine . . . splendid. (*He touches her neck, then kisses her on the ear.*) It's funny how funerals always make you appreciate what you've got.

Close up on HARRIET.

HARRIET. That's right.

Interior: Main Staircase – Day

We cut to shoes being hurled out of the bedroom, followed by various other objects. HARRIET *emerges out of the bedroom.*

HARRIET. Where the hell has he put all the cases? (*She really yells.*) Where are the bloody suitcases? (*Calling down the stairs.*) Louise! Theresa! (HARRIET *stares down the bannisters, the only person she can see is* LILLIAN *sitting below in her usual place on the half landing.*) Where is everybody?

HARRIET *moving with great, furious determination, despite her heavy size, she climbs onto a box on top of her chair to reach some high cupboard on the second landing on the staircase.*

She totters perilously on the chair, seemingly completely oblivious of the danger, the box on the chair at an alarming angle. HARRIET *gets the cupboard open.*

There's the bloody thing! (*Pulling at her suitcase, buried amongst other suitcases in high cupboard.*) If Hugh has locked it . . . ! (*She pulls at case trying to get it out.*) What a ridiculous place to put a load of suitcases.

The phone begins to ring.

(*Calling out.*) Don't anybody answer that – don't you dare to try to answer that Lillian, OK. It's Hugh, I know.

She manages to pull the suitcase out and the rest of the suitcases rain down around her, smashing several ornaments below her on the landing, and causing considerable devastation in the passage.

HARRIET *gets off the chair, seemingly oblivious to the mess, and moves off with her suitcase.*

We cut to HARRIET *standing by the answering machine, playing back the message.*

(*Staring down at the machine.*) If he mentions . . . if he mentions the CAR just *once.* (*To machine.*) I warn you.

HUGH'S VOICE. Hello darling . . . this is Hugh, of course. Where are you? Are you in the bathroom or something? Why didn't you answer the phone? Sometimes you must remember to check if the volume on the ringer has been turned down. There's a little knob on the phone – do you see it? – marked 'Ringer'. Check it now darling, just move it sideways if you need to, that's right.

HARRIET *not moving, poised over the answer machine.*

Now, I'll be dropping by later this afternoon, because today is the day the car has to go in for its quarterly service, so since no one else can take it in – I'll . . .

HARRIET (*triumphant*). He mentioned the car! (*Calling down to* LILLIAN.) Did you hear? He mentioned the car! Right!

We cut to HARRIET *going through her wardrobe grabbing dresses.*

Then we cut to her by the front door, opening it. She is dressed in a long coat, holding two suitcases, LILLIAN *is staring at her from the half-landing.*

HARRIET *looks embarrassed for a moment, holding the suitcases.*

I am just popping out – just for a moment.

LILLIAN. I think I could pop out too . . . be nice to pop out.

HARRIET (*impatient*). I'm only going round the block, to the shops.

LILLIAN. I'll pop out to the shops too.

HARRIET (*sharp*). I'm not going far – you'll see. (*Their eyes meet.*) If you *have* to come – come on then! Get ready! Hurry up!

Exterior: London House – Day

HARRIET *and* LILLIAN *walking along the cars in the drive.* HARRIET *carrying three suitcases now, including* LILLIAN'*s battered one, with its labels from the mental hospital still on it.*

LILLIAN *clasping the bag she had at the beginning of the film.*

HARRIET. We ought to take my car of course – because we're only going to the shops, take five minutes at the most. (HARRIET *stops at the Daimler.*) But what the hell!

She starts unlocking the Daimler.

Where are you going?

LILLIAN *has decided to sit in the back, stands determinedly by the back door.*

You don't trust my driving I see . . . I can't think what gave you the idea. Reckon you're safe there do you? I wouldn't bank on it. (*As* HARRIET *gets behind the wheel.*) We're only going for a little spin, that's all.

Exterior: Street outside London House – Day

Cut to the Daimler setting off at speed down the road – HARRIET'*s foot really down on the accelerator, she scrapes the car on a bollard as she goes round the corner, quite a bad scrape, more of a gash along the wing.*

LILLIAN *sitting in stately splendour in the back, rolls her eyes at* HARRIET'*s febrile driving.*

HARRIET. Don't know what you're doing making faces like that . . . If you're going to be back-seat driver you can walk! Or you can drive! Can you drive?

LILLIAN. I don't remember.

HARRIET (*smiles*). Very convenient loss of memory! I'm going to start making a list of those, the things you choose not to remember. (*She puts her foot down again.*)

Anyway Hugh is already going to kill me for that, for that scrape . . . he will cut me up into little pieces . . . it's the only thing that really enrages him . . . maybe he'll wait for the baby before he starts dismembering me because of the car. (*She smiles.*) I don't know. I'm not at all sure which means more to him . . . (*Her tone suddenly serious.*) It's going into service today, this car . . . I mustn't forget. I must get it back in time for that. We're only going round the block after all, we got plenty of time . . .

Exterior: Confectionery Shop – Day

Cut to the car pulling up outside a large confectionery shop.

HARRIET (*looking at* LILLIAN *in the back seat*). Do you want to make a pig of yourself?

Interior: Shop – Day

Cut inside the posh confectionery shop with HARRIET *buying a large pile of chocolates, luxury boxes stacked on top of each other.*

HARRIET. How much? £60!

There is a very poker faced middle aged shop assistant serving them.

You got it Lillian?

LILLIAN *shakes her head.*

LILLIAN. I have no money at all.

HARRIET. Oh yes of course I forgot. (*To shop assistant.*) She doesn't believe in paying for things.

LILLIAN *is pointing at something.*

What do you want? What are you pointing at?

LILLIAN. I would like that bird please.

LILLIAN *is pointing at a large chocolate chicken.*

HARRIET. You want that! It's about the most hideous thing in the shop. You sure? (*To assistant.*) She's been away for a long time, you have to forgive her a few things.

LILLIAN (*very determined*). I WANT THE CHICKEN. (*Sharp.*) PLEASE.

HARRIET *totally unabashed in front of the shop assistant.*

HARRIET. Didn't people bring you things like this in the loony bin? I would have thought it was just the sort of revolting present people would have shown up with.

LILLIAN. Apples. I got nothing but apples. Very unripe apples too.

Poker-faced assistant watching, getting agitated now.

HARRIET (*turning*). We'll take the ghastly chicken too then.

Exterior: London Street/Interior – Car

LILLIAN *sitting in the back in splendid isolation nibbling little pieces of chocolate off the chicken.*

HARRIET *also munching chocolates compulsively as she drives.*

HARRIET. We'll just go round the block once more then . . . OK?

HARRIET *watching* LILLIAN *in the driving mirror.*

Was that a nod? I wish your nods would get a bit bigger. You're quite capable of saying yes. (*Slight smile.*) What's it to be? Once more round the block?

Pause.

LILLIAN (*quiet*). Yes.

Exterior: Country Motorway/Interior Car – Day

Cut to wide shot of the car travelling through rolling countryside in Oxfordshire, ripe landscape, they are travelling along the motorway.

HARRIET. What do you think of it so far Lillian?

LILLIAN *sitting in the back, the chicken is now half eaten.*

Our little spin! Do you think it's time to go back? (LILLIAN *licking her fingers, of chocolate!*) Or do you think we should go round the block one more time?

The red petrol light is flashing on the dashboard. HARRIET *is oblivious to it, she just doesn't see it.*

(*Smiles.*) Could have a picnic if we wanted, do a spot of fishing. I haven't the slightest idea where we're going . . . isn't that marvellous?

Red light flashing, then becoming permanent.

(*Warm smile.*) I wanted to show you there was still some country left, that it wasn't all swallowed up while you were in the bin.

LILLIAN *glances briefly out of the window.*

I suppose last time you were here, this was full of nice young boys in boaters driving about in their jalopies making honking noises at each other. Just country lanes and . . .

LILLIAN *grabs her arm from the back seat.*

What on earth are you doing Lillian? What are you poking me for?

LILLIAN. There's a nice light that has come on down there. The red light, see . . . does it matter?

HARRIET *sees the red warning light.*

HARRIET. Oh Jesus Christ. The bloody petrol, got to get off this road – or we'll be smashed up by juggernauts.

There is a juggernaut behind them, HARRIET *watches it looming up close to them.*

Where the hell is there a bloody turn off?

HARRIET *takes the next exit off the motorway.*

(*To car.*) Come on, come on, don't run out, get us somewhere, OK! (*Furious.*) It's typical of Hugh, he never fills the car right up, he's too mean, he has some theory or other about wastage, the last two litres in the tank being unnecessary or some shit.

She hits a bollard at the side of the road, as she is saying this. The car is now badly dented.

They are travelling down a quieter country road. The engine stops.

The car has stopped Lillian, we're out of gas.

HARRIET *turns off the road, and lets the car slip gently down a dirt track in a wood, until it comes to a halt. The light is just beginning to close in, evening falling fast. Silence, the car has stopped.*

It looks like we're here for the night.

LILLIAN (*quiet surprise*). You want me to sleep here?

HARRIET. Yes! I'm in no condition to run around the country with petrol cans, but you can if you like. (*Slight smile.*) Can change a wheel or two if you like, and give the engine a little tuning.

LILLIAN, *not amused, sitting in the back.*

If we are here for the night, can you do me one very big favour? Don't bang tin plates around, *please.* You can take one night off can't you? OK?

LILLIAN *throws a box of chocolates at her.*

Lillian, don't do that. You have to behave yourself. There's no room for you to do anything else. Understand?

LILLIAN *throws another box.*

Lillian please! It's not my fault we're here and there's nothing else we can do.

LILLIAN. I'm not meant to sleep outside.

HARRIET. I don't care what you're not meant to do.

LILLIAN. It's not allowed, it's forbidden.

HARRIET. You're not in the home now for chrissake! And this is what happens when you're not. OK? OK? I'm going to have a cigarette now too.

LILLIAN *coughs in protest.*

If that's you acting, it's very bad acting. I know I shouldn't but I deserve one. And we can feast on chocolates, nothing else to eat here.

HARRIET *lies back in her seat but is hit in the side of the face by another box of chocolates that* LILLIAN *has tossed from the back seat.*

High shot of the car with its lights on now, in the middle of the wood, as the night closes in.

Interior: London House – Hall and Landing – Evening

Cut to HUGH *walking back into his house.*
LOUISE, THERESA *and* DOMINIC *are all standing waiting for him in the hall.*

HUGH. Louise, Theresa, what's the matter!

LOUISE. We found the place like this. When we were out . . . something terrible's happened.

HUGH. Terrible, what you mean? Where's HARRIET?

HUGH *running up the stairs, to the second landing where the smashed china is all over the floor, the shoes thrown everywhere, and the chairs lying at crazy angles.*

LOUISE (*calling up*). Miss Harriet, and Miss Lillian are not here.

HUGH. Not here? (*Staring at the broken things.*) Have you called the police? We must call the police at once!

LOUISE *has come up the stairs, kneels and starts to pick up things.*

Nobody touch anything. (*Sharp.*) Put that down at once, Louise. Everything must stay exactly as you found it. (*He picks up the phone.*) They took Lillian as well . . . Jesus. (*He dials emergency services.*) Can I have the police please!

Exterior: Wood – Day

Cut to the morning light. LILLIAN *stretches in the back of the car, then peers through the window at the early morning wood.*

She stares out at the winter trees, and the undergrowth. She's surprised to see two boys staring back at her, from the darkness of the wood, then another pair, then another, we see there are nine or ten kids, both boys and girls, standing in the shadows. They are dressed in an amalgam of clothes, post punk, weird clothes. Two of them have dirt smudged on their faces, like they have camouflaged themselves like combat troops.

They look quite frightening as they stare back from the edge of the trees. To LILLIAN's *eyes they appear to be like Amazon Indians in a forest, their faces half obscured by branches, wild exotic people.*

One of the boys moves closer. HARRIET *opens her eyes, slumped across the front seat, to see these faces staring at her through the windscreen. She yells out and jumps up.*

LILLIAN *gives the boy a ferocious look from the back seat, and he retreats slightly.*

HARRIET. Lillian for chrissake, we've got to get out of here. (*She instinctively tries to start the car, then remembers.*) Come on, out, out . . .

The kids standing, a little distance off, wary of this odd couple they see emerging from the car.

HARRIET *gets out, and in her haste her dress gets caught in the door, and part of it is torn off.*

(*Furious.*) That's all I need! About to get murdered and look what happens! Come on Lillian let's get out of here.

HARRIET *takes the suitcases. With difficulty, they move away watched by the puzzled kids.*

(*Shouting back at them.*) Plenty of chocolates in the car, they're all yours! (*An afterthought.*) And the *car* for that matter!

HARRIET *turns to* LILLIAN *who is moving very slowly, not trying to rush at all.*

LILLIAN. Who are those natives?

HARRIET. Natives! Not quite. Just kids living rough . . . in these pockets of woods between the motorway. Nobody disturbs them here, obviously. (*Watching the kids close round the car.*) The wildlife of the area . . .

HARRIET *stops behind a bush.*

Anyway I got to change if I'm going to have to hitch, I've got to look respectable.

Exterior: Wood – Day

We cut back to the car, the kids are falling on it ravenously tearing at the seats, grabbing the remaining chocolates, smearing them on the upholstery, tearing out the radio cassette, the cigarette lighter, the telephone, the whole car being devoured. They also tear out some of HARRIET's clothes from the one suitcase she was forced to leave behind.

Exterior: Country Roadside – Day

Cut to HARRIET *sitting looking resplendent in the fine Ascot-like dress, sitting on her suitcase, with* LILLIAN *next to her sitting on another suitcase.*

In front of them is a strange telecommunications tower.

HARRIET. Lovely spot isn't it?

LILLIAN *calmly sitting on her suitcase, watching the tower.*

LILLIAN. It's quite nice here.

HARRIET (*lightly*). Yes, well we know how fond you are of staring at blank walls Lillian, but I'd like to move on.

LILLIAN *staring at the strange tower, and all its electrical antennae.*

LILLIAN. When does that work?

HARRIET. What do you mean?

LILLIAN. When does it work?

HARRIET. I don't know. All the time. I don't know. It's telephones or a listening thing or . . . God knows.

Lorry appearing, moving down the road towards them.

HARRIET *hitches with a languid movement of her thumb. Lorry passes and stops.*

Got one. (LILLIAN *looks dubious.*) It's not great, OK, I know. But girls like us can't be too choosy. Come on.

Interior: Lorry – Country Road – Day

In the cab of the lorry, Scottish driver, HARRIET and LILLIAN. Lorry driver studying them, with an amused smile.

LORRY DRIVER. And where are you two heading for?

HARRIET. I don't know, that's an exceedingly good question. (*To* LILLIAN.) Which way are we going?

LILLIAN *nods in the direction they are heading.*

It's OK, we're going in the right direction. (HARRIET *smiles a radiant smile at the driver.*) She hasn't a clue of course – but that doesn't matter.

Exterior: Modern Hotel – Day

Cut to the lorry moving into the forecourt of a large Holiday Inn-style modern hotel. The lorry moves in amongst the Mercedes and BMW's parked outside.

HARRIET (*calling down from the cab, with great style,* LILLIAN *peering next to her.*) Porter – get us out of this vehicle please.

Interior: Hotel Reception – Day

We cut to HARRIET and LILLIAN at reception checking in. HARRIET looking down at the form she has to fill in. HARRIET is full of provocative, dangerous energy.

HARRIET. Name? (*To* LILLIAN.) What are we called? (*She looks at the reception clerk.*) What are we calling ourselves?

(LILLIAN *about to reply.*) No don't answer that, it's alright.
(*To clerk.*) Only kidding . . . we're Mrs and Miss Dickens.
(*Indicating* LILLIAN.) She's my mother, she's the Miss. (*As*
HARRIET *fills up form.*) I'm giving her a holiday.

RECEPTION CLERK. That's nice. There's lots to see in this
area as I'm sure you know.

HARRIET. There'd better be. She hasn't had a holiday for over
fifty years.

Reception clerk looks startled, then recovers his cool.

RECEPTION CLERK. Really, that's (*searching for the right words*)
that's rather a longer pause than most of our guests take
between holidays. (*He smiles.*) I hope we'll make up for it.

LILLIAN *staring at the airport-lounge-like interior.*

HARRIET. You bet we will, we'll make sure of that. (*Picking up
the plastic key-card.*) What's this?

RECEPTION CLERK. Your door key.

HARRIET. This is a key Lillian. You see they look like this now.
(*Dangerous smile at reception clerk.*) What entertainment have you
got? We want to sample everything. We're looking for pleasure.
You understand.

RECEPTION CLERK (*eyeing them warily*). We have some
dancing, of course, and all the usual amenities. (*Pushing leaflet
at them.*)

HARRIET. Hear that Lillian. (*Looking at leaflet, sharp smile.*)
Saunas . . . disco . . . adult TV channel, that means porno
channel. Great. We were hoping for one of those, weren't we.

RECEPTION CLERK *staring at them, rather alarmed.*

Exterior: The Wood – Day

*We cut to the wood, the abandoned Daimler, the place is swarming
with police, and police cars in the wood. Blue lights flashing, officers
moving through the undergrowth, finding the piece of* HARRIET's *torn
dress. We see it being put in a plastic bag. We see policemen examining*

*the car, with its torn seats, the havoc the kids have caused, that looks
as if some violent act has taken place inside the car, the stains of
smashed chocolate, and the broken windows. We see beyond the trees
there is a small lake and police frogmen are getting ready to search it.*

Hotel: Bedroom – Day

We cut to LILLIAN *sitting on one bed in the hotel room just making
herself comfortable,* HARRIET *lying on the other, sweating profusely.
It is a horrible room, full of plastic looking fittings. But trying to be
luxurious.*

HARRIET (*is shouting down the phone.*) You can't believe how hot
   it is in here, we spend £120 quid a night – and we get punished
   like this, roasted alive! What you mean switch it off – I can't
   switch it off, there's nothing to *switch* . . . this is the fifth time
   I've called, . . . you better bloody send somebody. The
   engineer's gone home? Then find another one. (*Slams down the
   phone.*)

Self-mocking smile.

I suppose I deserve this. . .

*She climbs off the bed, with difficulty, feeling her pregnancy, her
size.*

Come on – let's do what rock stars do (*she smiles*) wreck the
place. . .

*She moves over to the heater . . . which runs along the wall with a
grid along the top. Trying to find a way of switching it off. She's
really sweating. The plastic key, which she's waving around in one
hand, slips through the grid running along the top of the heater.*

(*Smiles*). Great! Might as well get everything I want to get rid of
   – and feed it into this heater. (*Starts burrowing in her bag.*) Get
   my dental reminder . . . in it goes. Some pills. The car keys.
   Some of Hugh's credit cards. (*Laughing.*) Shove my whole life
   down there, and maybe stop this heater as well! Clog it up.

LILLIAN *watching* HARRIET's *febrile mood, as she shoves things
down the heater.*

LILLIAN. Are you not feeling well?

HARRIET *looks up in surprise.*

HARRIET. She asked me! She spoke! (*She smiles.*) Thank you for inquiring, but I'm fine. Really. And isn't this great? Nobody in the whole world knows where we are. I have no idea why I find that so exciting right at this moment, but I do.

Interior: HUGH's House, Dining Room – Night.

HUGH *eating just a bowl of soup,* DOMINIC *tucking into a large plate of steak and potatoes.*

HUGH (*quiet*). Your mother will be fine . . . I know it. I'm going to keep talking about it, because I think we should.

DOMINIC. Yes, Daddy.

HUGH. It's a kidnapping and God knows anything can happen, but I do feel it will be alright . . . in the end.

DOMINIC (*calmly eating*). Will you pay the ransom?

HUGH (*sharp*). Dominic! It hasn't come to that. Of course I will, if that's what's required.

DOMINIC. Yes, I think you're right to do that. You're not insured of course but –

HUGH (*sharp*). Dominic!

DOMINIC (*unperturbed, eating his steak*). – But that doesn't matter. I hope the police look around here, that's where they should be concentrating their effort . . . in a lot of cases kidnap victims are held very close to where they were kidnapped, maybe as close as half a mile. I hope they realize that.

HUGH. I'm sure they do Dominic – if it's true.

DOMINIC (*cross*). Of course it's true.

HUGH. OK, I've made a note of it. (*Trying to sip his soup.*) I hate to think of your mother frightened, Lillian will be alright. Probably doesn't realize what's going on, but your mother, . . . she always thinks she likes drama and . . . but she doesn't.

HUGH *unable to bear the sight of* DOMINIC *eating with such relish any longer.*

How can you sit there eating like that? (*Sharp.*) It's unnatural.

DOMINIC (*looks up calmly*). You *sure* they really have been kidnapped?

HUGH. Of course. The signs of the struggle here, the condition the car was in when they found it. Nobody saw anything here but –

DOMINIC *finishing his plate, chewing the last piece of meat.*

DOMINIC. After dinner we should look at the clothes that were taken . . . there will almost certainly be a clue there. Don't you think? (*He looks up at his father.*)

Interior: Hotel Bedroom – Evening

Cut to HARRIET, *leaning over the washbasin in the bathroom, splashing cold water over her face, again and again, almost feverish movements.*

LILLIAN *is sitting at the end of the bed, staring at the television, the nine o'clock news, the sound is on quite softly. An item of world news gives way to a piece of home news.*

As LILLIAN *is sitting on the bed she idly begins to draw on the wall with some of the leftover chocolate eclairs they have had for tea.*

'Police are investigating the disappearance of the wife of city financier, Hugh Ambrose, from his Kensington home on Wednesday night. There were signs of a struggle in the house, and Police later found Mr Ambrose's car in a wood near the M40 in Oxfordshire. Pieces of women's clothes were found in the undergrowth nearby' etc. . . .

As the images come up to illustrate this news story, the house, the car in the wood, LILLIAN *is watching fascinated, but gradually getting impatient when there is no mention of her.*

LILLIAN. Where am I?

Then a picture appears of both of them. A flattering, recent picture of HARRIET, *and a completely unrecognizable one of* LILLIAN, *and the commentary continues.*

'A second person has also disappeared from the family home on the same day, Miss Lillian Huckle an elderly aunt of Mr Ambrose, recently returned from a period spent in hospital.'

LILLIAN'*s eyebrows raise at this description.*

The picture of her shown on the screen is several years out of date, and looking like a police photo, of a mad axe-woman.

LILLIAN *stares with some digust at the picture, and then stirs herself, to attract* HARRIET'*s attention.*

LILLIAN *gets off the bed, as the commentary continues to roll with a short interview with the policeman in charge of the investigation.*

She goes into the bathroom, where HARRIET *is by the basin.* LILLIAN *tugs at her sleeve.*

LILLIAN. Come and look what's on the machine . . . come and see. You must see it.

HARRIET. What's this? What's the matter with you?

HARRIET *moves into the room, but the item has changed by then, the news has moved on to an item about the Royal Family.*

HARRIET (*looking at the picture of the Queen*). I had no idea you felt so strongly about the Queen, Lillian. (*She smiles.*) I've learnt something about you . . . (*She turns.*) NOW, I'm going to get us dressed for tonight!

Interior: Hotel, Corridor – Night

LILLIAN *and* HARRIET *come out into the hotel corridor in their evening dress. We see them in long shot coming towards us,* HARRIET *looking dazzling, and* LILLIAN *in one of* HARRIET'*s dresses, looking very striking too. They move along the passage, with a little difficulty.* HARRIET *because of her great size.*

HARRIET. OK, let's slay them shall we!

Interior: Hotel Dining Room – Night

HARRIET *and* LILLIAN *enter the dining room, large modern dining room with cascading glass decorations, and a dance floor. Two or three couples are taking part in a modest genteel disco. There is a band dressed in red and white playing versions of current hits.*

The head waiter approaches HARRIET *and* LILLIAN *as they stand on the edge of the dining room surveying the scene.*

HEAD WAITER. I am sorry, madam, but the food is all finished.

HARRIET *(startled).* Finished?

HEAD WAITER. 9.30. It finishes at 9.30. It is now *(he holds up his watch)* 9.35 .

HARRIET. I don't believe this – you are not serving food any more? *(Loud.)* Can you believe this place, Lillian?

HEAD WAITER. Everything is finished – except the carvery. *(He indicates joints of meat, in a side area marked 'The Great British Carvery')*

The carve yourself meat . . . that is available.

HARRIET *(tottering slightly, being made to stand like this.)* Carve yourself?

HEAD WAITER. Yes – it is meant to be shut too . . . but I think we can make exception. *(Glancing at a manager standing in the shadows.)* Can we let these ladies use the carvery?

HARRIET *(dangerous smile).* We're being punished Lillian – it's like Hugh planned this – and said 'do this to them' – *(She moves.)* OK. *(She grabs two plates.)* They've asked for it, let's do it!

We cut to HARRIET *carving the meat, hacking into it, giant slices onto both plates. A ferocious amount of meat.*

They're going to see some champion carving tonight . . .

Then we cut to LILLIAN *and* HARRIET *moving to their table, the only one that is empty, moving across the dining room, with their plates absolutely groaning under the weight of the meat, the size of the portions.* HARRIET *has taken most of the Great British Carvery with her.*

People can't help but look, glancing stares, as HARRIET *and* LILLIAN *cross the dining room.*

(*To* LILLIAN, *indicating the stares.*) Don't take any notice of them, they're just jealous.

They reach the table.

(*Sinking into her seat.*) Let's tuck in shall we?

She picks up a piece of meat in her hands and starts really ravenously tearing into it, oblivious of the people watching.

LILLIAN *sits watching her for a moment. She is smiling at* HARRIET.

(*Looks up at* LILLIAN, *meat over her chin.*) Well, I'm glad I've made you smile.

Interior: HUGH's *Bedroom – Night*

Cut to HUGH *and* DOMINIC *sitting on the floor of the bedroom, clothes spread out all around them.* HUGH *holding one of* HARRIET's *dresses.*

DOMINIC. You see . . . her favourite dresses have gone, haven't they? Of all her clothes . . . (*They stare at the cupboard with all* HARRIET's *many dresses.*) . . . she's taken four of her favourite dresses. (DOMINIC *watches his father.*) If she was being kidnapped – it's unlikely that would have happened, isn't it?

HUGH. You sure those are her favourite dresses?

DOMINIC. Yes Daddy – even I know that, it's what she wears for really special occasions. And she's taken her own suitcase too – that Italian one she likes.

HUGH. The police say they must have made them grab a few things before they took them out . . . But maybe they let Harriet choose her best clothes . . . gave her time to pack.

DOMINIC. That wouldn't make it a very normal kidnap would

it? Mummy wouldn't take her best clothes for that. (*Calmly.*) It would be unnatural. (*He smiles.*) Even for mummy.

HUGH (*sitting on the floor with* DOMINIC). Maybe. So what do you think it means?

DOMINIC (*suddenly looking embarrassed*). I don't know Daddy – what do you think?

HUGH. It can't mean she just left (*he gropes for the words*) left of her own free will. (*He gets up, pacing.*) I mean it would be terrific of course – I mean it could be she's safe, but . . . (*Silence, he looks at* DOMINIC.)

DOMINIC (*quiet*). I can't imagine why either Daddy. (*Genuine.*) I've been thinking, and I can't.

HUGH. Maybe Lillian did something to her. I'm beginning to think it was a mistake bringing her here. (*Suddenly urgent, picking up the phone.*) I'm going to get the police to bloody find them! Now it's time we took a hand. They've had long enough!

Interior: Hotel Dining Room – Night

Cut to the disco, the plump figures of the prosperous of the district, dancing, some even gyrating, on a Friday night. There is a birthday party group with party hats just finishing their meal, and some coloured lights are playing across the walls as the band plays.

HARRIET *pours the last drops out of a wine bottle into* LILLIAN's *glass. It is obviously not the first bottle they have finished between them.*

HARRIET. I know you don't like me still.

LILLIAN *shakes her head.*

What does that shake mean? Do you mean you do or you don't?

LILLIAN. It's getting better.

HARRIET *smiles.*

HARRIET. Of all the people to be lumbered with – you come out of that hospital after 50 years and you get stuck with me! (*She drinks, her tone light but direct.*) A spoilt ex-bit part actress, who couldn't act, and is a lousy mother. (*Amused smile, totally without self pity.*) Worthless, not an idea in my head, no real knowledge, no political views, (*she smiles*) nothing. (*Her tone changes.*) I know that.

LILLIAN *watching her, a little nod.*

(*Sharp laugh, touching her a moment.*) Don't be in a hurry to contradict me will you. (*She looks down for a moment.*) Hugh thinks I'm a kind of scatty flighty creature – doesn't he – that has to be trained, *really* trained, but who sometimes can act being hostess of his dinner parties surprisingly well –

LILLIAN *lifts empty wine bottle, catches a passing waiter by the sleeve, presents him with the bottle.*

LILLIAN (*to waiter*). More. Lots more.

The dancers dancing, the music loud.

HARRIET. I mean Hugh is a good man. He is. (*She laughs.*) That is what's so terrible – he tried so hard, for both of us, he really tried. He is the perfect provider, he has a strong sense of family and all that (*she smiles*) and we loathe him for it.

LILLIAN *smiles at this too.*

You see you do! (*She looks at* LILLIAN.) It's unforgiveable isn't it?

HARRIET *is tapping the cutlery to the awful music, the dancers swirling round them, very close to the table.*

(*Lightly.*) The English trying to be sexy. (*She laughs.*) It's really gruesome, isn't it?

We cut to the dancers, then back to LILLIAN *and* HARRIET.

I bet you must be thinking I wish I'd stayed away for another fifty years!

As they talk the plump dancing couples do take on a ludicrous, complacent, grotesque appearance.

HARRIET *leans across the table as the dancing couples get closer and closer, jostling their table, brushing nearer and nearer, as they spread out from the main dance floor.* HARRIET *shoves her fork into a couple of bottoms that come too close, she gets some very strange looks.* LILLIAN *smiles, delighted at this. But* HARRIET'*s face, complexion, is looking different, flushed and ill, although her eyes are shining.*

It's very unattractive I know – to be so full of hate. (*Staring straight at* LILLIAN'*s eyes.*) Is there anything worse, any worse feeling in the world than hating the child you're about to have? . . . and not really knowing why. (*Matter of fact.*) That's terrible isn't it? And I have no excuses . . . One of the simplest things isn't it, that feeling, (*looking at* LILLIAN) and it really is quite horrible (*quiet*) scary . . . And I don't know what to do about it. (*She leans very close to* LILLIAN.) What about you, going to say anything to me?

LILLIAN. I don't think so.

HARRIET. Why not? It's just us here. (*Catching hold of* LILLIAN'*s wrist, very direct.*) You despise us all, I know, don't you? (LILLIAN *looks away.*) Yes you do, you can't forgive, why should you? (*Direct.*) You can only start again, that's the only thing you can do, Lillian. Start again from scratch. But I haven't got the guts to do that. I'm much less brave than you were. (*Loud.*) I can't even leave him for chrissake, can't make myself. (*She pours* LILLIAN *some more wine.*) *You* did what you had to, you followed your feelings, or instincts or whatever you'd call it. I'm guessing you did of course – because you won't tell me about it!

LILLIAN *looks away.*

(*Warm smile.*) Didn't exactly get you very far did it! But that's something else. . . .

LILLIAN *stares across at TV.*

Are you listening to me? I may be drunk but I demand your full attention, Lillian. I *know* I shouldn't be drinking, for the baby, but I *am.*

As she has been saying this, LILLIAN *is pointing. Above the bar, behind the barman is a television, and their pictures are on the television again, in a brief resumé of the news. Seen through the haze of the dancing figures, nobody but* LILLIAN *seems to notice.*

(*Following* LILLIAN's *pointing.*) If I wasn't so pissed, I'd say they look a lot like us.

The picture has gone now.

LILLIAN. It was. We're wanted on the television.

HARRIET. Wishful thinking Lillian! You want to be famous do you?

A MAN *comes up to the table, looking down at her as dancing figures jostle round the table.*

MAN. What a dance love? (*He is leaning close.*)

HARRIET. You won't want me when I stand up.

She stands up, she looks enormous now. She moves with much heaviness like a tank towards the man, he backs away, and the dancers try to avoid her, spreading out before her, a little exclusion zone breaks out around their table. HARRIET's *bulky shape moving to the music.*

(*Calling down to* LILLIAN *as she moves.*) I have a funny feeling of getting bigger and bigger. (*She laughs.*) Swelling by the minute . . . (HARRIET *calling down to* LILLIAN *indicating the scene in front of them.*) Think Lillian, what would happen if we did go away for another fifty years, what would we come back to? How would it look then?

They both stare at the cramped, plump dance floor under the cascading glass.

You know what I think, we'd come back to exactly this! The muzak might have changed of course. (*Staring at them.*) But not much else.

Interior: HUGH's *House – Night.*

HUGH *on the phone,* DOMINIC *by his side, with maps spread out of England.*

HUGH (*to the police on the phone*). We have drawn up five areas here, radiating out from where the car was found – and a list of the hotels, and (*snaps*) are you listening to me? I want you to check the following hotels, yes hotels – because I believe my wife and my ageing aunt under whose influence I believe she's acting – are staying normally – in some hotel. People should be able to spot them a mile off! And we're going to find them tonight – do you understand that, (*savage down phone*) because you've made a proper balls up of it so far. FIND THEM.

HUGH *slams down the phone, looking at* DOMINIC, *sudden doubt in his voice.*

I hope you're right about her favourite dresses. I've only got *your* word for it.

DOMINIC. Yes Daddy. Don't worry, I'm right.

HUGH (*more dangerous*). Then where the hell are they?

Interior: Dining Room and Dance Floor – Night

Cut to the dining room deserted covered in crushed streamers and squashed party hats. Two diners left, HARRIET *and* LILLIAN, *and all the waiters standing round impatiently.*

HEAD WAITER. Come on please – come on ladies! Time for bed.

HARRIET. We'll come when we're ready! (*Her face close to* LILLIAN, *urgent tone.* HARRIET's *face very red and looking strange, but she seems oblivious. She puts her hands either side of* LILLIAN's *head.*) Lillian . . . tell me, what it was like being shut away like that. I often think about it. The whole of the war for instance, must have been just a series of distant rumbles and bangs which nobody explained to you, was it? Going on somewhere far away. Tell me. Just *one* thing about it all. I know it's difficult for you, I know you find it hard to talk.

LILLIAN. I can't.

HARRIET (*strong*). Yes you can.

LILLIAN. I can't, Harriet . . . (*She turns her head.*)

Pause.

It was, every little year, every little year that went, I shut things away some more . . . because I'd shouted so much and then one day you can't anymore.

And you just grow smaller and smaller, tighter . . . until even very ordinary things become so . . . difficult. It all stops working . . . (LILLIAN *looks up, straight at* HARRIET.) Will that do?

HARRIET (*laughs*). Was that the real thing, Lillian? Or just manufactured for me? I can't tell with you!

LILLIAN *stares back not indicating either way.* HARRIET *touches her.*

That's what I like about you, I really do. (*She touches her.*) You're so hard, Lillian.

Interior: Hotel Lifts – Night

We cut to LILLIAN *standing by a row of modern lifts pressing the buttons.*

HARRIET. Come on let's climb, otherwise we'll be here all night. Somebody's hired all the lifts for tonight, probably have to pay extra to use them!

A couple of girls pass them.

GIRL. Oh yes, didn't you know you ought to have special lift vouchers.

The two girls giggle and exit.

HARRIET (*very sharp*). Thank you.

HARRIET *and* LILLIAN *move off towards the stairs.*

They begin to move up the stairs.

We cut to them on a landing about to move up the second flight. When HARRIET *suddenly collapses, breathing rapidly, her blood pressure very high, she looks very ill.*

HARRIET. I can't move Lillian, I don't know what's happening, I can't move.

LILLIAN *begins to move down the staircase.*

LILLIAN. I will get them, stay there.

HARRIET (*recovering her normal self for a second*). I'm not going anywhere am I!

Interior: Hotel Corridors – Night

LILLIAN *now suddenly on her own, wandering down a passage, in the enormous hotel, looking for somebody. There is a faint sound of music, she follows it, and opens a door. There is a small private party going on in the 'Waterloo Suite'. A crowd of people laughing inside, there is a man inside the door, one of the guests.*

GUEST. This is a private party, you can't come in.

  LILLIAN *suddenly finding she can't get the words out quick enough.*

LILLIAN. You must. (*Very urgent.*) You must . . .

GUEST. Sorry, private party. (*He closes the door.*)

  We see LILLIAN *in a maze of identical passages, moving past the hideous decorations.*

Interior: Hotel Staircase – Night

We cut back to HARRIET *lying on the stairs breathing with difficulty. She tries to move down the staircase on her bottom with great difficulty.*

HARRIET. What's happening to me? Who's doing this? Did Hugh arrange this too? Did you? (*Really loud.*) Is this what I deserve? (*Screams.*) Is it? Could somebody . . .

  She collapses at the bottom of the steps.

Interior: Hotel Reception – Night

We cut back to LILLIAN *who has found the reception, the reception clerk and two young women standing there. The receptionist casually chatting them up, as he watches TV simultaneously, 'Pillow Talk'.*

FIRST GIRL. No, we haven't finished for tonight. You shut down so early, we're going off to the Casablanca, it's new, just opened.

LILLIAN *gets up to the desk.*

LILLIAN. You must come at once.

RECEPTION CLERK. Just one moment madam.

LILLIAN. You got to come . . . (*Fighting the words out.*) She's, she's . . . she's on the stairs. She . . .

RECEPTION CLERK. You want the stairs madam? I'll be with you straight away.

LILLIAN. You'll be with me now!

RECEPTION CLERK (*rolling his eyes at the girl, as much as to say 'I've got a right one here'.*) Excuse me a moment, now madam is it your key that you've lost, or your room?

LILLIAN. Bloody fool. (*She makes a jabbing movement, with the heavy ashtray that is on the desk, she hits the fire alarm, not hard, but hard enough to break the glass, and the whole hotel is ringing with alarms.*)

Interior: London House – Night

HUGH *sitting in the shadows in the darkened sitting room,* DOMINIC *watching. During his speech,* HUGH *is flicking magazines off the coffee table with an increasingly sharp flick.*

HUGH (*his tone suggests he believes* DOMINIC). If you're right . . . if she and Lillian went off (*his voice rising*) leaving *NO NOTE*. (*He makes it sound a threat.*) I will never *understand*, never, how she could. . . . (*He stops.*)

DOMINIC (*watching in the shadows*). No Daddy.

HUGH. To cause all these problems, all these people running around the country, it's even been on the television.

DOMINIC. You have to expect that.

HUGH. On the national news for chrissake, everybody will have heard about it. (*Loud.*) What *do I tell them*? What? (*Furious.*) She never showed any sign at all that something was wrong.

DOMINIC. No Daddy.

HUGH. None. Just remember that! (*He begins to pale.*) My God, she'll have to explain a lot . . . these last weeks till the baby is born, she'll never be out of my sight. I mean it! (*His voice really tense, really loud, his face full of incomprehension.*) I want her back for godsake! (*He turns, he cries out.*) Dominic – I want her here!

Exterior: Hospital – Night

We cut to HARRIET *being carried out of an ambulance now barely conscious, and rushed through the glass doors, her face distorted in pain.*

Interior: Hospital – Night

HARRIET *being sped along hospital corridors on a trolley, doctors running alongside and nurses, the whole atmosphere surrounding an emergency case.*

Interior: Operating Theatre – Night

We cut to HARRIET *being taken into the operating theatre, the whole ritual of an operation spinning into life, the oxygen mask, the equipment closing around* HARRIET. *Her face looking very different, very ill.*

Hospital Corridors – Night

A DOCTOR *emerges into the passage, where* LILLIAN *is standing.*

DOCTOR. You're the person with her are you? (*The* DOCTOR *looks at* LILLIAN.) Are you the patient's mother?

LILIAN. I . . . (LILLIAN *hesitates, not wanting to be told to leave if she gives the wrong answer.*) I, not . . . not quite her mother I . . .

DOCTOR (*looks knowingly at a nurse standing there*). OK, we'll deal with that later. Now, she's suffering from Eclampsia, that is rapid rise in the blood pressure, general swelling, excess water in the body . . . it is extremely dangerous for both the mother and the child, so we have to get the baby out, *NOW*.

LILLIAN. I must see her.

DOCTOR. I'm afraid that's impossible, just wait here.

LILLIAN (*with real force, not trusting him*). I must see her . . . (*She thinks quickly.*) I have something to give her. (*Stamping.*) I *must* see her.

DOCTOR (*sharp*). You don't seem to understand that young woman could easily die, now stop wasting our time, and wait over there.

He takes her firmly by the arm, and guides her forcibly across the passage. LILLIAN pulls away from that grip on her arm, automatically tearing herself away, she's been guided like that so often.

We see a sudden torrent of thoughts, flashbacks being unleashed. Like at the party, gradually gathering in intensity.

Flashback: Interior, Mental Hospital Corridor – Day

We see her as a young girl being guided down a passage, with exactly the same grip on her arm, each time she moves her arm, the grip tightens. We don't see the man who is holding her, just the shoulder, and the arm. And the grip tightening.

Flashback: Interior, Harley Street Consulting Room – Day

We then see the YOUNG LILLIAN in a large room facing two doctors, one a woman, across a smart consulting room. YOUNG LILLIAN is pacing backwards and forwards, remonstrating at them with real force.

YOUNG LILLIAN. You don't know what you're talking about, that's the trouble, and I *know* you don't. That's what you don't like.

And she moves across the room and tugs at one of the curtains, the large curtains come crashing down, the whole curtain rail.

Flashback: Interior Mental Hospital Office – Day

Then we see YOUNG LILLIAN *sitting across a polished desk, sitting bolt upright very much the same way we see her sitting opposite* HUGH *in front of the blackboard at the beginning of the film. A very correct male doctor faces her.*

DOCTOR. Now do you understand Lilly? The answers you give to these questions are very important. A lot rests on what you reply now . . .

We see a beady look in YOUNG LILLIAN's *eyes, determined to give deliberately perverse answers.*

DOCTOR. Who is the Prime Minister of this country?

YOUNG LILLIAN (*very deadpan*). A kind of monkey.

DOCTOR. What do we call a man that looks at our teeth?

YOUNG LILLIAN. A bloodthirsty man.

DOCTOR. What is the name of this country where we live, what do we call it?

YOUNG LILLIAN. I don't know. Black Island, some name like that. A place that you fall through.

DOCTOR (*writing*). Fall through?

YOUNG LILLIAN. Fall right through – and come out the other side.

DOCTOR. Why do you think you are here?

YOUNG LILLIAN. Because I'm cleverer than you . . . because I'm meaner than you, because I see through you, and it would be much easier if I wasn't around. (*She smiles sweetly.*) Wouldn't it? And because you don't feel anything. (*She suddenly tweeks his hand across the desk.*) You don't feel this, or this, or this. Just like my father.

Flashback: Interior London House, Drawing Room – Day

We cut to close up of YOUNG LILLIAN *and the cousin* EDWARD *in their love scene on the nursery floor, a sensual erotic kiss, as they lie among the toys, it's as if it's a continuation of the moment that burnt out to white in the party scene, in the middle of the film.*

YOUNG LILLIAN. They'll come soon, find out where we are. Can we stop them? (*Urgent.*) Stay with me? (*A passionate kiss.*) *Stay.* I can make you stay forever.

Flashback: Interior London House, Drawing Room – Day

We then see her facing her father, in front of a large ornamental mirror.

YOUNG LILLIAN. I want to explain why it's not possible for me to listen to you any more – it's because I've stopped believing.

FATHER. You're talking nonsense Lilly.

YOUNG LILLIAN. I can no longer believe you exist. I have lost my faith, I can't believe such a boring, small-minded, lumpy man can be my father. (*She stares into his eyes.*) So I've decided you aren't my father. You have ceased to be.

Flashback: Interior London House, Conservatory – Day

Then we cut to a conservatory, heavy with flowers and tea things, a scented place. And YOUNG LILLIAN *is being approached by a man and a nurse, talking to her in gentle tones.*

YOUNG LILLIAN. Get away from me!

A terrible fight ensues as they try to catch hold of her, tea things being broken and smashed, glass being smashed as the sharp face of her sister MARGARET *watches terrified, totally uncomprehending.* YOUNG LILLIAN *kicks and screams and when finally they have got hold of her, she picks up the nearest thing at hand, a pair of silver sugar tongs, and slices the man repeatedly across the face.*

Very quick images follow of YOUNG LILLIAN *in the institution*

*being held down, crying uncontrollably, then being examined by
doctors strapped down to a table.*

Then a shot of the OLD LILLIAN *being held down too in a chair,
followed by* GLADYS's *face approaching her with apples, and then
a room full of some of the relatives we saw at the funeral
approaching* LILLIAN *across a room, looking deeply embarrassed,
keeping their distance.*

OLD LILLIAN (*whispering to herself*). What a miserable bunch, I
had forgotten how awful they looked.

Flashback: Interior Mental Hospital, Cell – Day

And then the YOUNG LILLIAN *being shut up in a small room and
screaming passionately and repeatedly through the grid in the door.*

YOUNG LILLIAN. I don't know what's the matter with me, but
it's nothing compared to this place – what's wrong with all of
you. You can't even do this properly, (*screams*) can you?
Bastards. (*Screams.*) Bastards – DON'T DO THIS TO ME,
YOU BASTARDS . . .

*Her face ferociously crying by the grid. We stay on her – she screams
through the grid. Desperate screams, that shake right through her
body.*

Interior: Hospital Corridor – Night

We cut back to the present. LILLIAN *standing by a window in
profile, beginning to shake very slightly.*

Interior: Operating Theatre – Night

We cut to HARRIET *being operated on, close up of her face,
unconscious.*

Interior: Hospital Corridor – Night

Cut back to LILLIAN *by the window, staring at the traffic moving on
the night roads, and the office blocks lit up opposite the hospital. She
stares at this contemporary view, her body shaking.*

LILLIAN. I don't know what happened to all that time . . . it was just taken away . . .

In the corridor there is a woman of about fifty, sitting with two young children. She nods at LILLIAN, *not knowing what* LILLIAN's *talking about, but nodding pleasantly.*

I can't forgive, she is right about that you know . . . and to have to *start* again . . . (*Tears pouring down* LILLIAN's *face, but her voice is tough.*) It's a bit late . . . a little too late . . . and it's so tiring now . . . (*Her body shaking.*) It frightens me, it frightens me so much.

The woman in the passage smiles at her, nodding. LILLIAN's *body really shaking, then she turns.*

I don't want her to die. (*Loud, dangerous to woman.*) Do you hear? I DON'T WANT HER TO DIE.

Woman nods sympathetically.

I expect they'll bungle it up, don't you . . . make a bad job of it . . . better go and make sure they're doing it right. (LILLIAN *sets off down the passage muttering.*) They aren't doing it right. (LILLIAN *shuffling along.*) They'll make mistakes like they always do.

Interior: Operating Theatre and Corridor Outside – Night

We cut back to the operating theatre, doctors working on HARRIET *surrounded by machines,* HARRIET *buried amongst it, her face looking very small.*

Then we cut to LILLIAN *trying to enter the operating theatre, people closing round her, pulling her back, restraining her.*

LILLIAN. I *must* see her. I don't want her to die . . . I won't let them. (*Loud.*) I don't want them to kill her.

We cut back to HARRIET. *Her figure fragile among the blood and machines.*

Then we see LILLIAN *staring through the window in one of the doors at the back, watching intensely, apprehensively, every move.*

To her eyes the modern operating equipment takes on a futuristic, menacing aspect.

(*At first quiet, but growing more and more insistent.*) You do it right. You do it right. You hear me. Do you hear me. *You do one thing properly,* understand. YOU DO THIS RIGHT.

We cut back to the operating theatre, getting closer and closer to HARRIET's face. We hear her breathing on the sound track.

Interior: Incubator Room – Night

Then we cut to LILLIAN staring down, with a nurse beside her, at a tiny premature baby in an incubator, fragile, covered in wires, just clinging onto life. LILLIAN staring down at it with grave fascination.

Hospital Room – Night

We cut to HARRIET lying in a small cubicle room, nurse just coming out, LILLIAN moving up to the door.

NURSE. You can't go in there, now.

LILLIAN (*taking no notice*). Rubbish.

She goes through the door without looking at the nurse.

NURSE (*moving off*). I'm coming right back in a minute to get you out of there.

HARRIET (staring at LILLIAN, *quiet, Pause.*) There you are. They say it may live and it may not. The baby. I don't know if I want it. Still. Isn't that terrible?

LILLIAN. No.

HARRIET (*slight smile*). I could be dead apparently, nearly was.

LILLIAN (*staring down at her*). Yes.

Exterior/Interior: Hospital Entrance – Night

HUGH *arriving with* DOMINIC *marching through the electric doors with tremendous determination.*

HUGH (*to* DOMINIC). Stay there. (*Indicating seats.*) I need to do this on my own.

Nurses bearing down on HUGH *to stop him getting past reception at this unusual hour.* HUGH *brushes past them, walks literally through them, sending them scattering, and hitting a trolley that rolls into a wall with a crash.*

HUGH (*as he does so*). Out of my way ladies – thank you.

HUGH *marches on, out of sight down the passage.*

DOMINIC *sits coolly on a bench against the wall, stretching his arms along the back of the bench nonchalantly.*

DOMINIC (*to nurses*). Don't worry – he'll pay for any damage he does. (*Calmly.*) He's collecting my mother you see.

Interior: Hospital Room – Night

We cut back to HARRIET's *room.* HARRIET *moving with difficulty in bed, staring back at* LILLIAN *in pain.*

HARRIET. Jesus, it hurts.

LILLIAN *moves slowly towards her and leans over* HARRIET, *brushes her cheek clumsily with her mouth, a strange form of a kiss. She does this for quite a long moment, then moves away.*

HARRIET (*laughs*). What's that meant to be? (HARRIET *leaning back in the bed.*) So what the hell do we do now, Lillian? (*She laughs at herself.*) Listen to me – I'm asking *you* that.

LILLIAN. Yes! (*Watching her.*) I don't know why you're laughing.

HARRIET *leans back, slight smile.*

Interior: Hospital Corridors – Night

We cut to HUGH *marching down the corridors, now with a flotilla of doctors and nurses, surrounding him. They round a corner, and move towards us down another corridor, getting nearer and nearer* HARRIET's *room.*

Interior: Hospital Room – Night

We cut back to HARRIET's *room, just as* LILLIAN *is pushing a chair, or a small cupboard with great difficulty and effort so it bars the door, forming a kind of barrier. It requires a lot of effort from* LILLIAN *but she gets it into place.*

LILLIAN (*turns to* HARRIET). Go to sleep now. Go on.

LILLIAN *is by the door, staring out of the glass, standing guard.*

I'll tell you when they're coming.

Close up of HARRIET, *she smiles, her point of view of* LILLIAN *standing guard by the door, then she leans right back in her bed, and half closes her eyes.*

Interior: Hospital Corridor – Night

We cut back onto the corridor – we see HUGH *come round the corner with all the doctors and nurses bearing down on* HARRIET *and* LILLIAN.

Then we suddenly see apprehension and doubt come into HUGH's *face, into his eyes. His pace falters.*

For he sees LILLIAN, *standing guard, massively determined. A face he has to get past, staring through the glass directly down the corridor at him.* HUGH's *pace slows almost to a standstill as do the doctors and nurses round him.*

We cut to LILLIAN's *face, staring out at* HUGH *and us, in giant close-up, full of power, unmoveable, staring directly into us.*

Hidden City

Hidden City premièred at the Metro Cinema, London, on 24 June 1987.

THE CAST

JAMES RICHARDS	Charles Dance
SHARON	Cassie Stuart
ANTHONY	Bill Paterson
BREWSTER	Richard E. Grant
HILLCOMBE	Alex Norton
BARBARA	Tusse Silberg
SCHOOLMASTER	Richard Ireson
CURTIS	Saul Jephcott
BOYCE	Michael Mueller
YOUNG MEN IN TUNNEL	Stevan Rinkus
	Gerard Horan
MAN AT INCINERATOR	Chris Jury
MAN AT RUBBISH TIP	Cambell Morrison
MAN IN TRAM TUNNEL	Robin Soans
WOMAN TEACHER	Noreen Kershaw
GIRL AT FLAT	Ariol Goldingham
GUESTS AT DINNER PARTY	Helena Little
	Charles Millham
MANAGERESS AT HAIRDRESSING SALON	Michelle Copsey
WOMAN IN FILM LIBRARY	Jelena Budimir
WOMAN IN FILM DISPOSAL	Barbara Young
APPLICANTS AT HAIRDRESSING SALON	Michelle Collins
	Wendy Nittingham
JAMES RICHARDS AS A BOY	James Trigg
JODIE	Laura Welch

In Black and White Film:

THE WIFE	Brid Brennan
BLOND WOMAN	Katy Behean
YOUNG MAN	Jason Carter
INTERROGATOR	Vass Anderson
BURNED MAN	Anthony May
DIRECTOR	Stephen Poliakoff
PRODUCER	Irving Teitelbaum
EDITOR	Peter Coulson
DIRECTOR OF PHOTOGRAPHY	Witold Stok
PRODUCTION DESIGNER	Martin Johnson
MUSIC	Michael Storey

Introduction

As soon as it appeared likely that I was going to have the chance
to direct my first film, I started on a search. A search across
London for the locations, the unexpected hidden areas that I
hoped would give the film a texture, a view of the capital that was
as different as I could possibly make it from the conventional 'red
bus' London of scores of movies.

'Hidden City' is a mystery that winds its way across London,
and as layers of the central characters' lives comes away and are
exposed, so too do layers of the city. A seemingly bland and
neutral place on the surface, I wanted to show an increasingly
dark, secretive, even magical city underneath.

So to this end, early on in the process, I found myself several
hundred feet under Belsize Park, being escorted along two miles of
tunnels by a lugubrious 18-year-old boy. It was very cold down
there, although it was mid-summer up above. It was dark. And,
as the boy explained, it was frighteningly easy to get lost. All
through the tunnel, was a surreal collection of belongings and old
archives, stored in a seemingly chaotic jumble and covered in soot.
Apart from the thousands of boxes of personal papers, there were
architectural drawings of buildings that had never been built,
crates from liquidated companies, and dusty cans of film, ranging
from old features to show reels of commercials from the '60s, to
films that had been made but never shown. It is interesting to
speculate whether, in a decade's time, this same tunnel will be full
of British TV programmes that have fallen foul of the
Broadcasting Standards Council.

This particular tunnel was privately owned: anybody could
store whatever they wanted. And it was a revelation to me.
Because I soon discovered that there was a whole series of these
tunnels, dating from the '20s and the '30s, lying below the tube
line, burrowing through London, under Camden, Tottenham
Court Road, Clapham, Stockwell and many other places. And
several of them were true time warps that had been left totally
unchanged for decades.

Some had been used for billetting troops during the war,
packaged together in sweaty lines. You can still see the graffiti
written on the bunks as they waited for D-Day; ventilators, the

size of aircraft engines, now lying amongst the cluster of war time telephones; and notices saying that only the officers can use the lifts, everyone else must climb the several hundred stairs to the surface. And these tunnels all have three layers, like an ants' nest, going deeper and deeper underground.

FROZEN IN TIME

In one tunnel under Stockwell there is another, more recent, period frozen in time. A hippy commune colonised it and painted several hundred of the bunks in psychedelic colours. They lived below the surface for several years and indeed scraps of '60s ephemera are scattered along the tunnel floor, the only remains of a subterranean community that few knew was in their midst, and has now melted away.

I soon found myself becoming rather obsessed by these tunnels and kept on coming across new ones. Right up to the very first day of shooting I was still trying frantically to get into the romantically named Camden Catacombs.

One of the grandest tunnels the characters visit in the course of the film is the old Kingsway tram tunnel. But what could not be shown in the movie is the collection of seemingly innocent Portakabins that nestle in the belly of the tunnel. The cabins are full of working telephone lines, charts of London and the stench of old carpets. When I asked my guide on my first visit what they were used for, he told me that in the event of London being flooded, this is where everything would be run from.

Down in a tunnel! At the time of a flood! . . . I was incredulous as we groped our way in the dark over the tram lines.

'Oh yes, it's perfectly safe here, quite high up in fact. No problem.'

By the time we came to shoot in the tunnel, the GLC, which owned it, had gone. A strange and unreachable residuary body had sprouted up, which absolutely forbade us to film there. Days of argument failed to move them. We also found that part of the tunnel had been closed because it was riddled with asbestos, but simultaneously it had been upgraded in importance. No longer was it to run London after a flood but instead, in the event of a civil nuclear disaster, the nerve centre of the city would be in this decaying tram tunnel, in a cabin on one of the old platforms, surrounded by asbestos. Relentless pleading finally got us in there in the middle of the shoot but with strict instructions that under no circumstances could we film the Portakabins or even allow a tiny part of them to creep into shot.

'Hidden City' is principally about secrecy, the obsessive secrecy of English life. It portrays a London absolutely choc-a-block with secrets. A world of deep incompetence and some panic, in which trivial secrets and important ones are kept side by side, where so much classified material is shovelled underground that people have forgotten why it was classified in the first place, or even where the really important secrets are. A process that leads to menus from long forgotten banquets being stored and guarded for years while apparently vital documents are thrown on rubbish tips. And of course, from time to time, some of this confidential material bubbles accidently to the surface and is found blowing along Tottenham Court Road, or along a tow path beside the Thames, or in the middle of Wimbledon Common.

But not all the subterranean secrecy is connected with files and documents. While sitting alone in the fading splendour of Charing Cross Hotel, looking for another location, I fell into conversation with a neat elderly pinstriped man who turned out, like a lot of Londoners, to have an extraordinary fund of knowledge about the city. At one point he leaned forward and whispered, 'Do you know the Masons worship right under Piccadilly Circus? Just think of them being right under your feet next time you cross the road there.'

MASONIC RITUALS
It was an irresistible image, Masonic ritual going on directly underneath Eros and the Trocadero. So, because the Masons make a brief supporting appearance in 'Hidden City', I decided to try to visit these temples. After various negotiations a precise time was agreed when the temples were being cleaned. The entrance turned out to be through the large heavy doors in the sub-basement of the Café Royal. But beyond the door the temples were far more tacky and down-market than I had ever expected. Bright green neon notices like the 'Gents' in a local Odeon point to the Masons' robing room and the temples, which were quite small and smelt of damp. They did not stretch quite under Piccadilly

Circus but they do penetrate out under the pavements of Regent's Street. So, next time you walk up there, you will, if you time it right, be treading above the heads of bobbing senior policemen and cabinet ministers.

Furthermore, underneath the Masonic temples, even deeper down, is another unexpected layer of contemporary London, a series of old wine cellars that are let out for various Hooray parties and other select gatherings, forming a peculiar subterranean sandwich of clique activities.

During the early scenes of 'Hidden City' the character played by Charles Dance is trying to find some cans of missing film which have been thrown away, and which he's rushing to get to before they are destroyed. Researching the scenes led me to discover the astonishing world of waste disposal in London, the barges that set off down the Thames from Battersea, groaning with waste like something out of Dickens, the open rubbish tips, full of people crawling over them scouring for valuables, and the great incinerators, amongst the largest in the world, where one of the main dangers for those who work there is the illegal dumping of hospital waste, with bags full of flesh and hypodermic needles regularly turning up where they shouldn't.

Getting permission to film inside the incinerator complex was like trying to get inside the Ministry of Defence, and required months of negotiation . . . It turned out to be a place that had a regular stream of unexpected visitors. Officials from the Eastern Bloc and Israeli embassies would often drive out there with classified documents to put them personally inside the incinerator. Many afternoons, the place would apparently be alive with chattering Russians and Poles as the waste piled up around them and their official cars sat among the rubbish trucks.

The day we were filming there a group of policemen was standing disposing of several hundredweight of obscene material, individually feeding it into the fire. It was a strange scene: at one end of the vast central rubbish vat, a film crew with its director urging Charles Dance to climb into a hopper full of foul smelling waste; and at the other end, the vice-squad eyeing us suspiciously as they personally handled the obscene material.

One of the central locations in 'Hidden City' is a large government building where a variety of odd and secret events takes place. The building is partly based on a Victorian orphans' asylum in Wandsworth which, during the Second World War, was used as a place of interrogation, secret trials, and, it is said, torture and executions. The detail of exactly what went on there is still unknown but the building is now transformed into an '80s paradise of luxury flats, little high-tech media offices and dance studios. The whole patina of successful contemporary London has washed over the building, while its past remains unwritten.

A MYSTERY IN FRAGMENTS

This tension between life now and the past in London is also at the heart of the story of 'Hidden City', where a young woman brought up on video images becomes obsessed by a mystery contained in fragments of an old newsreel. The hard, detached eyes of the '80s start staring directly into London's recent past and what is to be found lying just underneath the surface.

If you stare upwards in London too, at, for instance, the weird collection of attic rooms that line the most familiar streets, like Oxford Street, surprising things can also be found. Some mysterious rooms situated high above Bond Street play an important part in 'Hidden City' and the composite building I created for the movie. For the exterior of this building, I used the old Guildhall School of Music, a crumbling nineteenth-century pile just off Fleet Street. It has been empty for a long time and its interior was too dangerous to shoot in, unfortunately, because it has a romantic Jacobean-style central staircase and a magnificent theatre about the size of the Royal Court, with its red plush seats still intact and its curtains half-raised.

So we filmed the interior inside the old St Pancras hotel, above the station, another building that was taken over by the government and now lies empty. A sad place of endless corridors and evocative hotel bedrooms. While we were shooting there, I was told by officials about another complete station that lies beneath St Pancras. It was bricked up at the end of the last century, with its platforms, waiting rooms and buffets all still there, another time capsule waiting to be opened.

In fact, once you start scraping at the placid exterior of London, there is no end to the stories that float up about forbidden tunnels and lost buildings. One such story concerns the luxury hotel suites under the Strand, built during the First World War for guests frightened of the Zeppelin raids, and now bricked up, completely land-locked under the street. The story may be pure fantasy (I was unable to find them) but it does raise the marvellous image of whole sections of another city being down there, which you could travel through without ever coming up, from the Savoy-like splendour of the Edwardian hotel suites to the hippy commune, then along the underground rivers, past the Victorian buffet and the Masonic temples, to the nuclear disaster centre.

In 'Hidden City', Charles Dance's character goes on a journey that takes him from his initial complacent state, where he feels that neither life nor London can surprise him, to being plunged into events and into a landscape that he finds new, vivid and totally unexpected.

I hope the movie captures some of this sense of wonder, the dark and unpredictable side of the city and what is going on inside it.

Richards (Charles Dance) conducting
his research into young people and television

The woman (Brid Brennan) in the black and white film
is dragged through the streets

Richards meets Sharon (Cassie Stuart)
at the entrance to the old tram tunnel

Curtis (Saul Jephcott) goes into the tunnels
under Oxford Street to search for the film
Richard and Jodie (Laura Welch) find themselves
on the run through the eerie night streets

Richards and Sharon search the rubbish tip
for the missing can of film
Richards and Jodie discovering London at night

Opening sequence: Exterior: Canals – Day

A moving subjective shot down the canals, cutting through the forgotten pieces of London, sliding down the narrow waterways, trees tilting over dark water. We move both through leafy residential areas, and strangely deserted urban landscapes, dissolving from one to the other under the credits, the camera sliding just above the water. Branches and boxes, pieces of debris floating past, early autumn leaves and pieces of flotsam, alternately beautiful and decaying atmosphere, ending in a shot moving down the last stretch of a canal, tall black Victorian walls on either side, and then out into the blinding light and noise, and the wide open space of the Thames.

As these shots have slid into each other under the credits, there is a sense of the camera exploring, of being pulled further and further into the heart of the city.

Interior: Institute: Seminar Room – Day

Cut to the faces of 19 children aged about ten and eleven, watching an American TV space series on individual monitor screens. The children are formally sitting at desks, as if in class, in the middle of a large modern seminar room, steel and glass fittings, high windows with the curtains down, the room in semi-darkness. The children enthralled one moment, fidgeting the next, glancing at each other and giggling, eyes wandering all over the room and then back to the screens. Each of the children has a pad of paper and a pencil in front of them as if about to take an exam. One boy, with large eyes, is concentrating very hard and making notes.

A woman SCHOOLTEACHER *in a polka dot dress is moving in front of them in the semi-darkness, as the soundtrack from the monitors blares out ferociously and incongruously.*

The Space TV programme suddenly ends on all the screens simultaneously.

The TEACHER *pulls back one of the curtains, letting in a shaft of daylight, sound of heavy rain ouside.*

As the curtain goes back we see RICHARDS *standing in the shadow watching the children, a man in his late thirties or early forties, a very*

*watchful, contained manner, beautifully dressed in a discreetly
fashionable way. His manner exudes a sharp intelligence, a cool,
authoritative, rather formidable confidence.*

The TEACHER *addresses the class with brisk cheerfulness as they look
up from their TV screens.*

TEACHER. Now I want you all to keep just where you are, and
   to keep watching your screens just as you have been, because
   there is a second interesting film for you to see, some of you
   may even find it more interesting.

   RICHARDS *irritated by this as he watches from the corner.*

   It's about a piece of history, our history, the abdication of one
   of the Kings of England, Edward VIII and then Mr. Richards
   (*she smiles at him*) who has invited us all here, will have a few
   questions to ask you so you may write down anything that
   comes into your heads, if anything does, that strikes you as
   important.

As she says this, RICHARDS *is surveying the faces of the*
CHILDREN, *some fidgeting in their seats, but most are staring
excitedly and expectantly at the blank screen, eyes rapt, ready to
consume what they are shown.*

RICHARDS (*gliding from the corner into the centre of the room, facing
   the kids, he murmurs to the* TEACHER). Not a bad group this, 29
   kids, 17% black, 4% Asian, 79% white . . . (*Slight smile.*)
   Almost perfect.

The monitor screens come alive again, we face the CHILDREN
with RICHARDS, *for a moment we cannot see what they are
looking at, the* CHILDREN *seem to be reacting strangely, looking
at each other, odd noises are emanating from the monitors,*
RICHARDS *immediately surprised, watching the model* BOY *pupil
with the huge eyes who at first looks up at them as if they've let him
down, and then begins to writhe around in his seat in an
embarrassed way.*

RICHARDS *has moved forward and is staring down at the child's
monitor screen, and then at all the monitor screens. They are all
showing a black and white government information film for farmers*

about breeding cattle during the war, shots of cows pouring towards the camera wriggling their heads, shot of a bull mounting a cow, with a voice over, in plain BBC tone talking about when a bull reaches sexual maturity, and how many cows it can be expected to service at one session.

(*Dangerous smile.*) Jesus, not again . . .

RICHARDS *rips a plug out of a socket, all the monitors flick off, the sound moans off.*

Interior: Institute Corridors – Day

Cut to RICHARDS *moving down one of the glass passages of the Institute, glass portholes in the ceiling, futuristic architecture now beginning to decay and leak and look very fragile, heavy rain splashing on the glass, water spattering through, half way down a large puddle has formed forcing people to wade through it, as they use the passage.* RICHARDS *sweeps down the glass passage, in a stormy, furious mood, past doors suggesting the research nature of the building . . . in the opposite direction a small* MAN *in a lab coat is moving down the passage, carrying a cage with some small birds in it, brilliantly coloured red and green parrots, he waves in greeting to* RICHARDS *as he scurries past,* RICHARDS *shouts after him . . .*

RICHARDS. Somebody ought to do something about this
    passage. . .

The WOMAN TEACHER *is nervously following* RICHARDS, *not certain what to do . . . a reverse shot of the* CHILDREN *bunched up at the end of the passages, staring bewildered after them as the rain plays heavily on the roof.*

(*As he moves.*) This is not going to happen again. . . !

Interior: Richards' Office – Day

Cut to RICHARDS *in his office, a cool, completely ordered interior in pale blue and grey. Small windows, tall walls, files are immaculately arranged round the wall, crisp office furnishings, with just an extra touch of elegance in what* RICHARDS *had added, a computer, typewriter and word processor, a video machine and television, a line of pencils on his desk, a packet of brown Ryvita half eaten. A self-contained world.* RICHARDS *is sitting at his desk, on the phone, we cut into the scene when he is in mid-flow, the television and V.H.S. is on, playing the offending tape, the cows moving on the screen.*

RICHARDS (*cool, controlled tone, but formidable*). This is the second time it has happened and that is twice too many, no . . . no. (*Quiet.*) I don't understand I'm afraid. I would have thought it was rather a simple matter of sending me the film I asked for . . . not a guide to breeding cattle in Suffolk in 1941. It should not be beyond your competence. . .

The camera has moved round, to reveal the cattle playing on the screen, RICHARDS *watching them out of the corner of his eye.*

(*Slight smile.*) Yes . . . may I make one small suggestion – whoever was responsible for this cock-up maybe after today . . . they really oughtn't to be working for you . . . fire them, yes that's what I mean, that might be a bright move.

Interior: Film Library – Day

Cut to a dark shadowy, shabby room, part of a film library, long movable shelves stacked with cans of film, a notice on the wall 'Absolutely all smoking prohibited in this area'.

A MIDDLE-AGED WOMAN *in a chintzy dress is sitting on an elderly swivel chair, her tone very apologetic.*

MIDDLE-AGED WOMAN. Yes I agree . . . I see your point, absolutely . . . I think we may have to do something . . . not unlike what you are suggesting.

We are observing her from the point of view of somebody standing in the semi-darkness among the rows of films, the person moves circling at a distance from the MIDDLE-AGED WOMAN, *we see the person's eyes, green eyes, watching, listening, from among the shelves. She lights a cigarette casually in the shadows, we cannot see her face, but we can see the notice behind her.*

She moves out from among the shelves and walks idly away from us, a girl with long red hair, nonchalantly touching the sides of the shelves as she goes.

Exterior: RICHARDS' *Garden and Canal – Day/Evening*

Cut to us moving along the dark canal water. Similar to the opening shot, early autumn leaves just beginning to fall, an orange plastic bag floating like a large jelly fish, but this time the shot is brief, and sweeps us round a bend in the canal, with laughter and conversation ringing through the early evening air towards us. The shot reveals houses with gardens tilting right down to the water's edge, a dinner party is in progress. Evening light mixing with the light spilling from the house and illuminating the small garden, lush flowers and shrubs, all around.

RICHARDS *sitting at the head of a table outside a Georgian terraced house, at the other end is* ANTHONY. *The same age, late thirties, early forties, unmistakably the sixties generation, now mellowed into success, he is with a young girl* MELANIE, *dressed in a very short skirt, and an expensive blouse,* BARBARA *is sitting opposite her, a dark haired woman about 40, shy good looks, watching across the fruit brûlée as they dip into their sweets, the last person at the table is a young pale-faced student, a bearded silent type, constantly looking from* BARBARA *to* RICHARDS *and back down to his food; he has a private superior smile, continually flickering. On the surface, a happy dinner party, but as the following snatches of conversation slide into each other we feel the tension underneath, the strained, fragile atmosphere.*

ANTHONY. There were crates and crates of them . . . I had to flush them all down the drain. The smell was unbearable, left alone with an entire bathroom full of oysters. (*Giggling.*) It was completely surreal.

BARBARA (*to student*). Have some more.

She scoops the fruit brûlée, raspberries and peaches sliding onto the boy's plate; as she does so she indicates RICHARDS.

When we were married we never stopped eating I seem to remember, especially dessert, we became pudding junkies . . . (*Looking sideways sharply.*) Isn't that right dear?

We cut momentarily to the other side of the canal, almost as if they are being observed from the other side of the water.

We cut back to the table, into another conversation.

RICHARDS (*his precise, confident manner, effortless, charming smile*). That's relatively easy, the longest living animal ever recorded, the lake sturgeon at 145 years.

ANTHONY. A fish!

RICHARDS. The tortoise is second at 124 years, man is third at 117, the turtle fourth at 88 years . . . and the tape worm has been known to live for 35 years!

ANTHONY (*smiling, bantering tone*). Yet another useless fact. (*To MELANIE.*) As you may have guessed there is little James doesn't know.

STUDENT *picking at the fruit brûlée and smiling to himself. BARBARA looks up, she sees a girl, SHARON, standing on the bank across the canal, staring straight at them, munching a hamburger. As BARBARA watches SHARON drops the hamburger, accidentally, and casually picks it up from amongst the dead autumn leaves and continues to munch it. As this is going on we hear ANTHONY's voice.*

MELANIE (*suddenly straight at RICHARDS, almost aggressively*). Aren't you writing a book? Will it be finished soon?

RICHARDS *flinches very slightly, a piece of debris floating down the canal past them as they eat, it catches his eye for a second, and then a movement on the far bank as if somebody was there, but then the impression goes.*

ANTHONY (*bantering on*). He's still researching of course – endless research – James is one of those people that everybody thought had become extinct, wiped out by cuts, but there he is with all the time in the world to spend gazing at kids who are gazing at TV, they all just watch the tele all the time.

STUDENT *shaking his head and smiling to himself.*

MELANIE (*straight at RICHARDS*). It must be fun.

RICHARDS. It can be.

Interior: RICHARDS' *Lounge – Night*

Inside RICHARDS' *house, a totally modern open plan interior inside the old house, again the cool elegant colours, there are also some startling large black and white framed photographs, low evening light, trees blowing behind glass picture windows, dark coffee bubbling as* RICHARDS *makes it.*

In one single shot we encompass the whole scene, ANTHONY *talking to* MELANIE *as we move from the bookshelves, past the* STUDENT, *to* BARBARA *and* RICHARDS *in the corner.*

The STUDENT *is sitting entirely by himself in the middle of the room, blatantly ripping off cigarettes and putting them in his pockets, then some chocolates, then some more cigarettes, smiling all the time to himself his private smile. His manner so blatant it is deeply embarrassing.*

MELANIE *is standing with* ANTHONY, *we see a row of* RICHARDS' *successful book 'INSTEAD OF SEX?' – The Attitudes and Appetites of the Young in the Eighties'.*

ANTHONY (*lowering his voice*). His last book was all about sex . . . when I say his last book, his only book . . . he became quite literally a statistician with sex appeal, he spent two years asking adolescent kids how much they knew about it. *Not very much* it turned out. It caused a minor sensation when contrary to popular belief, he *proved* that kids on the whole knew less about sex, or rather no more about sex than they did 30 years ago . . . (*Smile calling over to* RICHARDS.) Though how he managed to interview kids 30 years ago remains a mystery!

BARBARA *whispering to* RICHARDS, *looking at the horrible* STUDENT.

BARBARA. You weren't trying to pair me off with that creation were you?

RICHARDS *smiles.*

MELANIE (*moving over towards* RICHARDS). How long ago was that? How long since you finished your last book?

The question takes RICHARDS *aback, he hesitates for a second.*

RICHARDS (*slight smile*). Some people would say too long . . .

ANTHONY (*calling out*). Some people might be right!

Exterior: London Residential Streets – Night

BARBARA *and* RICHARDS *alone walking down the leafy, night streets, sudden exhilaration at being alone after the dinner party,* RICHARDS *plunging away from his own house, away at last from the guests,* RICHARDS *striding along in the night air,* BARBARA *having to run almost to keep up, the camera tracking with them but some distance away, they begin to move up the hill.*

RICHARDS. God that girl – everything she said seemed to be designed to cause maximum annoyance.

We are seeing them from a distance moving up the hill.

(*Striding up the night street.*) Anthony really picks them doesn't he?

BARBARA. Your discovery for me was even worse, what a horrible boy . . . he was desperately trying to work out what was going on between us . . .

RICHARDS (*looking around as he moves, swinging his jacket over his shoulder*). God it's hot for this time of year! That girl may be right of course, I am beginning to wonder if I'll ever finish my work . . . three years research that doesn't lead anywhere . . . I really don't want to start writing, second books are so difficult.

He kicks at a large, black, plastic dustbin that has been left out on the pavement, it bounces and rolls down the middle of the road, gathering speed, disappearing from their view.

They have got to the top of the hill, London is lying spread out below them, night lights, the hunched shape of St. Pancras station, the tawdry neon round Kings Cross flickering. RICHARDS *begins to move again. The mood darkening between them.*

BARBARA. Where are we walking to, love?

RICHARDS *starts slightly as she uses that term again, he is moving at a tremendous pace, the camera keeping its distance, as if they are being followed at a discreet distance.*

RICHARDS. Maybe I *should* have gone to America. (*Staring at the night lights.*) Next time there's an offer, I'm going, this is the blandest city in the world, and its getting worse, I'm beginning to hate it. No wonder I can't work here, there's no energy. . .

BARBARA (*nervous laugh, staring at the empty street*). We could always walk back. I could *stay* tonight, we could go back and clear up . . . neither of us wants to go to sleep.

RICHARDS *keeps moving as if he hasn't heard.*

RICHARDS. There are seven thousand more taxis in New York than there are in London.

BARBARA (*very sharp*). Good, maybe we'll bump into one of those tonight and I can take it.

RICHARDS. New York. (*Smiling to himself.*) Wouldn't that be nice.

London spread out below them.

RICHARDS *suddenly turns and looks back down the street, the camera stops moving too.*

BARBARA (*following his look down the empty street*). What's the matter?

RICHARDS. I thought there was somebody there that's all. . .

Shot of SHARON *standing in the distance down the street, holding a very large plastic bundle.*

He continues up the empty street.

BARBARA. You're in a terrible mood.

She catches his sleeve for a moment as she struggles to keep up.

We never used to walk anywhere you realize.

She suddenly stops him under a street light at the end of the street.

(*Sharp.*) I wouldn't mind staying the night. I'm not sure you heard the first time so I'm trying again . . . I'm pretty amazed myself that I'm asking, but I am.

RICHARDS (*staring at her face, rather harshly lit under the lamp*). I don't think that would be a good idea. (*He gives her a fond but embarrassed smile.*)

BARBARA (*sharp, angry*). No, you're right.

She moves rapidly away from him, and her necklace breaks, beads scatter over the ground, for a moment she scrambles around on the road picking them up.

It's only cheap rubbish, it doesn't matter, I used to wear this as a student, I don't know why I put it on tonight.

RICHARDS *is watching her, cut off from her, for some reason he makes no move to help her, just watching her in the road.*

BARBARA *throws the necklace into a dustbin in the garden of a house near where they are standing and then she marches off down the street, her hands deep in her pockets. RICHARDS watches her go for a second.*

Exterior: London Street – Day

RICHARDS *moving along the street confidently, carrying a black attaché case, a paper under his arm, red buses rumbling past, a bland central London street scene in mid-morning light. RICHARDS walking down the pavement near a large, crumbling block of mansion flats, the shot moving round from behind him, moving level with him and then past him, as if somebody is walking past him, followed by a wide shot of him confidently striding down the pavement.*

Suddenly an arm shoots out from a doorway, catches hold of him, and literally yanks him towards the doorway.

RICHARDS *finds himself staring at a young woman, SHARON of indeterminate age, she looks about 18 or 19. She has long red hair, very pale skin, and bright, slightly disturbing green eyes. She is holding a large bundle, wrapped up in dirty plastic which she is holding onto tightly with one hand, and she clasps him by the sleeve with the other.*

There is a peculiar, intense quality about her, she looks as if she hasn't slept for days.

SHARON (*staring straight at him*). I need your help.

RICHARDS (*astounded, angry*). What on earth do you think you're doing?

He looks down at his sleeve, the stitching on the shoulder of his jacket has split.

Excuse me.

RICHARDS *pulls away from her.*

SHARON. I'm sorry, I didn't mean to spoil your jacket, is it torn? I'll pay for it later.

They are standing in the doorway of mansion flats, decorative old style doors and a spacious interior beyond which a HALL PORTER eyeing them suspiciously.

(*Fixing him with an intense stare.*) But I *do* need your help. (*She instinctively holds onto him again.*) Spare me five minutes?

RICHARDS *moves off down the street. She pursues him and catches him in a doorway of a shop. Behind her head are row upon row of the same postcard, Beefeaters staring back at us.*

BARBARA (*slight smile*). How can you resist such an invitation, how many times has this happened to you before?

RICHARDS (*icily*). Could you let go of my sleeve please?

SHARON. Don't seem to have a great choice of postcards round here. (*Turning back to him.*) Mr. Richards I need you to do it.

RICHARDS (*surprised by the use of his name*). Have we ever met before?

SHARON. Aren't you curious? (*She indicates the street milling outside.*) You can walk down there now, and never know what it all was about. (*She looks at him.*) Or you can come with me.

RICHARDS *looks down at her.*

I might even buy you a cup of coffee.

Interior: The Cafe – Day

Cut to low-grade, greasy-spoon cafe, housed in a vast and surprising room, once ornamental walls now seedy, yellowing glass in the window, large freckled mirrors on the walls, smudged and dirty, air cooling fans, only one moving the rest broken. Pictures of the special offers; eggs and chips, hamburger and chips on the walls, tat housed in fading grandeur. The place is dark and dusty, glinting sunlight piercing across the room; hidden in the corner a couple of tramps and bag ladies drinking tea . . . couple of other elderly customers, smoking and loudly coughing the smoke into the dusty atmosphere.

We see the room in wide shot which is held, with RICHARDS sitting at a table with a check tablecloth . . . as SHARON approaches, her red hair falling untidily, carrying the coffee, a striking looking presence in these surroundings. SHARON standing for a moment staring down at him.

SHARON. You owe me a very big favour.

RICHARDS (*about to drink his coffee, stops*). I owe you a favour?

SHARON. Very definitely.

RICHARDS. I fail to see how.

SHARON. Do you? (*She is staring down at him.*) You lost me my job. (*Slight pause.*) They fired me because of you.

RICHARDS. Because of *me* – that is highly unlikely.

SHARON. Which didn't please me all that much, as you can imagine.

RICHARDS. Oh yes. (*Remembering.*) For the cows I presume. (*Looking at her.*) In that case it was more than justified.

SHARON (*moving closer, she is not sitting down, hovering over him*). Drink your coffee. Don't worry I am not going to attack you.

A tramp coughs in the shadows, rummaging for something in the bag he's carrying. RICHARDS catches sight of SHARON's reflection in the big freckled mirror, and the dark passages tapering off into the rest of the building.

(*Following RICHARDS' look.*) You like it here? – it takes a particular kind of person to know about a place like this . . . I used to work here for a bit. (*Suddenly.*) See that man. (*She's pointing out of the window into the street.*) You can see the masons scuttling down the back entrance to their temples where they do all that secret worship – there goes one now. I've seen a lot of famous people go scurrying in there. The temples are deep underground.

The information all flashes out of her in a second as an aside.
RICHARDS *is still watching the perfectly groomed city gent
disappear through the shabby back door* SHARON *pointed to, when
he realizes she's slid into the chair opposite him and is leaning
towards him.*

You see you owe me something Mr. Richards – and it happens
you can give me the assistance I need. (*Pause.*) I have to show
you something. (RICHARDS' *slight smile.*) What's that meant to
be? A dirty look . . . not very impressive, you'll have to work on
it more.

*Her abrasive manner is off-set by an extraordinarily warm smile that
suddenly appears in mid-sentence, and then the intense, possibly
paranoid manner returns.*

It's in here, what I've got to show you.

RICHARDS' *eyes moving from the old bag-woman sitting in the
shadows rustling her bags, pieces of paper going everywhere, to*
SHARON *holding her dirty plastic bundle, clutching it like holding
an infant.*

RICHARDS (*slight smile*). You've got it with you have you? How
convenient.

SHARON. Of course.

RICHARDS. You don't think it might be a good idea to tell me
what it is.

SHARON (*straight at him*). Certainly not. If you knew, you
wouldn't come.

RICHARDS. Come where?

SHARON. It's very near. It will only take you a few minutes –
then I'll put you back on the pavement where I found you.

Her intense febrile manner, suddenly she turns her eyes on him again.

Of course you're thinking this girl is a nutter. I don't blame
you. (*Slight pause.*) But I can assure you I am not. (*She smiles.*)
I'll prove it to you, if you come with me. (*Straight at him.*) Are

you going to come or not?

Exterior: The Cafe and Street – Day

Receding shot of the exterior of the building housing the cafe, large Victorian pile in central London, like an old hotel. SHARON leading RICHARDS away from it, SHARON holding her parcel, RICHARDS watching her with an intrigued expression.

Interior: Video Reproducing Factory – Day

The warren-like passages and rooms of a video reproducing firm, a large one, a totally different place to the small, quiet film library where we first saw SHARON. People moving professionally and busily, it is a strong contrast to the delapidated cafe of the scene before . . . the machinery, the screens, the kids operating the equipment, running off copies of domestic tapes, commercial movies, and specialized films, the covers of many different titles of films splayed around the room and passages, giving an impression of the amount of celluloid swishing around the city, a television is on in the corner receiving Russian television and another with television from the Middle East, we can see the satellite dish through the window.

We catch a glimpse of an unexpected group of people working here, not just the technologically adept youths, looking even younger than they are, but an older woman of mid-European extraction doing some paperwork, an American girl answering the phone, and an Indian girl watching six screens simultaneously checking for flaws in the tape. We hear snatches of jargon constantly, half in earshot behind all the following action. Everybody is working intensely hard, atmosphere of pressure and success, hard glinting place, very hot, one of the men is stripped to his waist, as he flicks in new tapes.

As SHARON moves through this world, people call out to her as she passes: 'You're not back again are you, God help us' and 'Take cover, Sharon is here. . .' etc. SHARON hardly acknowledges them. We also notice CURTIS a young man in a long coat despite the heat and rather unflattering spectacles, who SHARON does greet, and the head of the firm, BREWSTER, a tall man with a large round face and luminous green glasses, who SHARON avoids.

BREWSTER (*calling after her*). What are you doing here Sharon? Don't you get in anybody's way . . . or I'll throw you out. Five minutes that's all you've got. (*Calling after her.*) No point asking you to keep quiet because that's impossible.

SHARON *moves straight on, not stopping to talk to him. As she passes the girl watching the six monitor screens.*

SHARON (*to* RICHARDS). That's the job I used to do here.

RICHARDS (*watching her*). You seem to have worked just about everywhere.

SHARON. I used to work at a film library too, but somebody lost me that job!

SHARON *stops at a table at the end of the room and drops her parcel on it. She pulls off the sordid plastic bag, the object is wrapped in muslin like a large cheese, she unwinds the muslin until a rusty film can is revealed.*

You're going to watch this.

RICHARDS. A home movie is it?

His attention constantly being distracted by the movement and noise from the large room, the Indian girl watching the six screens.

SHARON (*following his gaze*). If you could stop ogling that girl, I'd be grateful and watch this please.

SHARON *laces the film on the Steenbeck herself.*

RICHARDS *is surprised to see it's an old film that has come out of the muslin. Some black and white images appear on the screen – the number of the film, and street scenes, library shots, of 1950's London.*

BREWSTER (*shouting in the background*). Have you got those off to St. John's Wood? We said we'd deliver 25 by lunchtime so you only have 20 minutes.

Various Library Shots of London in the fifties.

RICHARDS *looks away from the flickering old film, to take in the hurly burly of the main room. Through the following action, the noise from the tapes on the other machines intensifies, the sound of car chases, space flights, soft porn, providing a constant distraction, encroaching more and more.*

SHARON (*calling at him*). MR. RICHARDS, please watch now, this is it, you have to watch *NOW*.

Exterior: A School and Street – Day

A shot appears in the old film of a milkman unloading milkchurns from a horsedrawn milkcart at the entrance to a school in a quiet suburban street. RICHARDS looks at SHARON, then at the screen at this mundane fifties street scene, then back at SHARON in disbelief. She is watching with almost obsessive concentration, RICHARDS starts to look away, surveying the room for the exit, trying to ease himself away from this disturbed girl.

SHARON (*suddenly*). Can't you see! Look, look properly, look at the back, look at the background, can't you see what's happening?

Exterior: A School and Street – Day

RICHARDS' *point of view, we move in on the background during the static shot of the milkman unloading his churns. Behind him, in the corner of the little bland, suburban street, a woman in her thirties is being stopped by two men as she walks home, and after a moment is being seemingly pushed towards a car, a large Daimler, and then suddenly bundled into it her arms seeming to wave in alarm, it is all over in an instant, so fast one can't be certain what one has seen, leaving the milkman still unloading his milkchurns.*

RICHARDS (*watching with half his attention*). What are you trying to show me?

The noise from the rest of the room growing all the time.

SHARON. Keep watching . . . (*Sharp.*) Don't take your eyes off the screen.

Stock Shot Exterior: London Streets – Day

Another Newsreel street scene of London appears. Piccadilly Circus theatregoers, taxis, etc. . . . This is followed by a shot of a park.

SHARON (*as this shot appears*). Watch, watch now; watch the
   background always . . .

Exterior: A Park – Day

The shot is of a park with a man watering some plants. In the background, a group of people are moving down a broad path, a woman between two men, maybe the same woman is being walked, dragged along the path in the background, her body twisting, for a fleeting second her face turns towards the camera her mouth open, maybe crying for help, but it is gone in a second as she exits the frame, leaving us with just the man watering the plants.

Stock Shots of London – Day

More library shots of London as RICHARDS *glances at the Indian girl again.*

SHARON. This is the most important one.

Exterior: London Street – Day

In the final shot we see a man selling newspaper with a headline board saying 'By-Election Shock' seemingly the point of the shot, and then as we move close, right up to the image, we see the same bundled group of people, two men pulling this woman between them, for an instant, an instant we see, but RICHARDS *half misses because he's been glancing round the room, we see the woman latch onto some railings and hold on, her face partly masked by the railings, she appears to be shouting, a hand goes over her mouth, and she suddenly disappears from view, into a dark doorway which one can't identify. Again it is all over in a few seconds, leaving us with the man selling newspapers. The film finishes. There are a few empty frames of white as the last feet of the film play through.*

RICHARDS. So? Was that all you wanted to show me. . .

SHARON. Watch. . .

Black and White Caption

On the very last feet of the film comes the caption 'See also 'The Hedgerows of England'! *with an exclamation mark after it. Then it is gone. The film snaking round the spool loudly as it finishes.*

RICHARDS. And that's it is it?

SHARON (*excitedly*). Didn't you see. . . ? didn't you see the evidence of your own eyes? Somehow . . . a kidnapping has been recorded there, an abduction . . . It's all been filmed, maybe a murder. (*Loud.*) In the back of that old film . . . and it's been filed away for years among those London street scenes. (*Excited.*) Don't you understand that. . .

RICHARDS. I'm sorry, I didn't see that . . . I saw some people walking that's all . . . how did you want me to help you anyway?·

SHARON (*impatient, as if the answer's blindingly obvious*). You have to find the other film of course . . . the one it told us to look for, you have to help me find it.

RICHARDS (*amused smile, hardly bothering to conceal his disbelief*). Why can't you?

SHARON (*sharp*). I was about to tell you that . . . you saw what it was called, the film 'The Hedgerows of England'. I've looked it up at the Public Records Office – for some 'reason' it is not available until 2050, it is covered by the Official Secrets Acts and is being stored by the Ministry of Defence. (*Suddenly lets it flood out.*) I can't possibly get access to it – especially now I no longer have a job. (*Right up at him.*) But *you* could, an important writer like you, doing significant work, you can say you need it for research, you must have friends in those sort of places, *YOU* could find it. . .

RICHARDS (*unable to stop her flow, her intense, slightly disturbing manner*). Excuse me, I have to go, I'm sorry, I have somebody waiting for me, thank you for letting me see that, but . . . (*He pushes past her.*)

SHARON *raises her voice, shouting after him so the whole room turns round.*

SHARON. Wait. . . !

Interior. Factory – Day

RICHARDS *moving down the long tapering passage of the warren-like building, the passage is rather dark, low ceiling, outside the window a satellite dish is visible.*

RICHARDS *moving briskly trying to get out,* SHARON *suddenly appears at the other end of the passage following him.*

SHARON (*calling the length of the passage*). Where do you think you are going?

RICHARDS (*controlled*). I am trying to find the way out of this bloody place.

SHARON. You can't just run away like that – that's much too easy. It would be really simple for you to help me, you could do it in a few hours . . . I need you to do it.

A motorcycle messenger is standing at the end of the passage, a huge looming shape in leather, having a smoke, as he waits for a delivery.

RICHARDS (*up against him in the narrow passage*). You couldn't show me how to escape from here could you.

Motorcyclist indicates door leading to back studio.

SHARON (*calling after him*). Please, wait. . .

RICHARDS *glances back as he leaves passage.*

(*calling after him*). What have you got to lose?

Receding shot of her calling in passage.

Interior: Swimming Pool – Day

A very large indoor swimming pool with purple tinted water – a private swimming pool in the basement of a large office block.

As we cut to the lush purple pool a fat man in very brief trunks floats into view, floating on his back.

The pool is surrounded by a gallery with tables for people to drink and stare down at the swimmers. On this particular afternoon, apart from the fat man floating, a young girl in a bikini is swimming round the edge of the pool. As the sequence progresses, she swims in circles nearer and nearer the man floating on his back. Two young executives, fully dressed in immaculate suits, stand with their drinks right at the water's edge, gossiping.

RICHARDS *is sitting with* ANTHONY *up in the gallery, opposite each other, the purple water visible below them in the back of shot. They stare down at the action in the pool, the mood of familiar banter between old friends.*

ANTHONY (*looking at* RICHARDS). A perfect place for a voyeur to spend his life, don't you think, here.

RICHARDS. What's that meant to mean?

He is watching the stomach of the fat man, as he revolves in the water, his very brief trunks, the girl getting closer all the time.

(*Slight smile.*) What goes on in the bowels of a multi-national at 3.00 in the afternoon. (*Laughs.*) No wonder British industry is on its knees.

ANTHONY (*looking at fat man*). On its back, more like. (*Drinks.*) He's got his priorities right.

RICHARDS (*watching the fat man*). YOU, in a few years' time, (*slight smile*) maybe sooner.

ANTHONY (*indicating his torn jacket*). What happened to you?

RICHARDS. That? Nothing. (*Lightly.*) I was bitten by a mad dog, in the street. (*Long pause.*) A loony. (*Glaring down into the pool.*) I'm thinking of going away soon. A sudden holiday, I'm hungry for one I realized today. Maybe Mexico, the West Coast, a total change of scene, San Francisco . . .

ANTHONY. Really. (*Teasing smile.*) I'm sure your work can wait! God I don't like to think how long ago it was since we made out trip, to the West Coast. When was it?

RICHARDS. 18 years ago. No, no, 17 and a half.

ANTHONY (*cutting him off*). Don't put a number on it. Your passion for numbers.

RICHARDS (*looking at* ANTHONY'*s executive appearance*). And look at him now! Hardly a trace is there, (*self-mocking smile*) whereas I look exactly the same. (*Tone changes slightly.*) Anthony, you always know these things, there wasn't anyone in our year that ended up in the Ministry of Defence was there?

ANTHONY. Oh yes . . . at least a couple. Why? (*Slight smile.*) Do you need a travelling companion?

Below them suddenly a bleeper goes off in the pool, seemingly emanating from the fat man in very brief trunks, he immediately rolls onto his stomach and swims vigorously to the side and hauls himself out.

(*Turning back to* RICHARDS.) If you want names, there is Francis . . .

RICHARDS (*suddenly brisk, losing interest in the idea*). No, no . . . I've changed my mind. It doesn't matter, I don't need to know.

Exterior: The Thames – Day

Early morning shots of the vast barges carrying waste on the river, black bags being tossed down into them from a doorway somewhere, and then a shot of the barge moving towards us, bearing down on us, in the misty early morning light.

Interior: RICHARDS' *Office – Day*

RICHARDS *alone in his crisp well-ordered office. It's hot, his jacket off, a pristine clear sheet of paper waiting in the typewriter. A bead of sweat drops onto the clear empty page. A clock is ticking. He stares at his computer – at a mass of information he has called up. He stares at a tower of crisp notes and papers with a sign at the top saying 'Responses to the 'A' Team'. A poster of the 'A' Team stares back at him mockingly from the wall. They stare at each other.*

There is a flash cut of the flickering black and white image, the woman being dragged along the railings her face twisting round, and cutting back sharply to the empty page on the typewriter.

RICHARDS *leans forward, his movements very precise and picks up the phone.*

Exterior: Tram Tunnel – Day

Cut to wide shot of SHARON *standing against the black iron railings, in the middle of Kingsway, standing staring straight ahead, she is wearing a slightly shabby secondhand fur coat. She looks very pale in the early morning light, she stands still holding her parcel, a strange looking figure against the railings.*

We see her looking suspiciously at a solitary young man walking a dog watching her.

RICHARDS' *point of view as he approaches her against the railings.*

SHARON (*giving* RICHARDS *a surprisingly warm smile*). You're late. . .

RICHARDS (*sharply*). I am never late.

Staring down through the iron gates into the darkness.

SHARON. Had to come a long way have you?

RICHARDS. I think you know where I've come from, since you seem to have made a complete study of me already . . . wandering around outside my house . . . (*He looks at her, we can see him wondering what on earth he is doing there.*) Still got your parcel. . .

SHARON. Naturally. (*Lightly.*) Maybe you could stop looking at me as if I'm some kind of specimen for your research. (*She smiles.*) I don't think I'll fit into the right category somehow.

Down below in the mouth of the tunnel – a figure is waving to them, holding a torch. A small OLD MAN.

OLD MAN. The gate's unlocked. Come down! Come down!

They pass through the metal gates and down the broad ramp, running into the mouth of the tunnel.

RICHARDS (*as they approach the tunnel*). In fact there really is no need for me to be here at all, I just rang a friend of mine and told him the title of the film and he said of course I could have a look at it, no problems at all. I have a note from him.

SHARON (*immediately takes it*). I'd better have that – it could be very useful.

They reach the OLD MAN.

OLD MAN (*to* RICHARDS). Here you are – thought you weren't going to come.

RICHARDS (*slight smile*). Yes, it was a close thing. This is my assistant . . . (*He realizes he doesn't know her name.*)

SHARON. Sharon Newton, he's always forgetting my name, it's quite normal.

OLD MAN. It's the films you want to see is it?

The OLD MAN *immediately sets off into the darkness of the old tram tunnel that runs down the centre of Kingsway, the torch beam darting around across the walls. The* OLD MAN *is talking all the time, like a guide in a museum, exuding real pride in his tunnel.*

Last tram was here in 1953, the busiest station in the West End, the most popular station in London, people from the best hotels came down here, in their evening dress, travel to the theatres, celebrities came down here, film stars. . .

As he says this we see the gleaming old tram rails, shining out at them. The torch beam settles on a light switch, OLD MAN *switches it on, and a line of naked electric lights come on, lighting up the curve of the tunnel.*

Old posters still there, peeling, the platforms still intact, the name of the station up on the wall, a fifties time warp.

The fading poster shows two people dressed for a first night outside a theatre and a sign 'Maxims New Restaurant now open', etc.

RICHARDS *looks ahead down the tunnel.* SHARON *has moved in front, and is standing in her fur coat on the platform impatiently waiting, like a waiting passenger.* RICHARDS *as he stares at her imagines the ringing noise, the hiss and the bells of the trams.*

OLD MAN *is muttering on ahead of him, as they follow the tram lines, which are dotted by small white stalactites from the moisture, like toadstools. Along the wall are a line of boxes, piled untidily.*

RICHARDS *plucks a document from one of them, whose top has come off; he is surprised to discover it is merely the menu of a long forgotten official banquet stamped 'confidential'.*

RICHARDS. Incredible place. There must be so much low grade confidential material . . . nobody's had time to sort it all. Just dumped it down here . . . (*he smiles*) and the trams ran right through here once.

SHARON (*showing no interest in the trams*). Be a great place to hide out if you were on the run.

RICHARDS. I'll bear that in mind next time it happens to me.

The noise above their heads, which has been building through the sequence, of feet and traffic, moving above them, is increasing all the time, we hear the full swell of it.

OLD MAN (*calling up*). The beginning of the rush hour.

A flutter of litter suddenly coming through, above one of the old side exits, dropping down towards them.

Get rubbish thrown on our heads all the time!

He has turned on the second light switch, the main part of the tunnel lights up, stretching ahead of them.

In the far distance instead of tapering off into darkness, it is blocked off by a wall of boxes and mail bags stacked up, right in the distance, like a huge ball of paper at the end of the tunnel. Between them and the ball of paper the ground is covered in little white pellets.

(*Waving at it*). Don't worry about that it's only rat shit. (*Pointing at the tower of paper.*) Paper and documents from God knows when, they ought to burn it all, nobody's ever going to look at them again! (*He laughs to himself and moves forwards.*) Now the films are here! It's the driest part of the tunnel, and so we keep them just here. . .

He shines his torch along the wall, they follow the beam. There is nothing against the wall except some empty boxes lying on their side.

They've gone.

SHARON. Gone?

OLD MAN. Yes . . . somebody's taken them. They must have moved all the films without telling me.

RICHARDS. When was this?

OLD MAN. It must have been last week, because I was here the week before. Maybe I've forgotten something, maybe they were going to be moved, maybe they told me, more secure place, better conditions for them. (*His torch beam moving along the wall.*)

SHARON. Where would they have gone?

OLD MAN. Gone to the shelter in Tottenham Court Road of course, they've got quite a collection down there, more secure you know.

SHARON. Can you get us in there? Can you arrange it? Is there anybody there now?

OLD MAN. Maybe. . . If it's Tuesday or Thursday.

RICHARDS (*sharp*). Now wait a moment, there's no question of me going there now.

SHARON. Please, just be there, until they let me in . . . (*Looking at him.*) I need you to make it look respectable.

RICHARDS (*looking at her in her moth eaten fur coat*). I'll drop you off there, that's all, nothing else. . .

Interior: Lift and Tunnel – Day

Cut to old lift doors sliding across their faces and clanging shut, the lift surrounded by darkness.

RICHARDS, SHARON, *and two pimply* YOUNG MEN *in smart grey suits and carrying a large bunch of keys each.*

1ST YOUNG MAN. Hold on tight – we're going a long way down.

A loud rumble as the lift shakily descends. We peer at them as they disappear into darkness.

RICHARDS (*as they sink down the lift shaft*). How long does it take to get to the bottom?

They come out in a maze of deep passages, marked with signs and wartime lettering.

Thousands of old army bunks stretching as far as the eye can see, now stacked with papers and boxes.

The dead kitchens where meals were served and the dead showers and lavatories still visible. A strange chair marked 'Do Not Touch' dangles from the wall.

1ST YOUNG MAN (*moving as if he was a librarian among the bunks*). What did you say the number was 204. . .?

SHARON. 2047.

1ST YOUNG MAN (*rattling his eyes*). Should be in R Section – (*Grins to himself.*) I can never find R Section. Nobody comes to look at any of this stuff usually! (*Slight smile.*) We don't get disturbed down *here*.

The 2ND YOUNG MAN *is behind* RICHARDS *as they move through the subterranean passages.*

2ND YOUNG MAN. You don't know what this place was do you?

RICHARDS (*sharp smile*). But you're going to tell me.

2ND YOUNG MAN. 15,000 US troops were stored here at night, during the war. (*Loud.*) 15,000 at a time! (*Points at wall.*) Can still see their finger marks . . . waiting for D Day or whatever it was called.

1ST YOUNG MAN. And nobody knew they were here. Popped down here at 4 o'clock in the morning.

SHARON *moving through this world, oblivious to what they are being shown.*

2ND YOUNG MAN. It was used during Suez too – during the

Suez business – wasn't it Mike?

1ST YOUNG MAN (*not looking round*). Yeah, and nobody knew they were here then either.

2ND YOUNG MAN. May have been used at other times of course – but we haven't been told.

1ST YOUNG MAN. No! (*To* RICHARDS.) Did *you* know all these tunnels were here – running under Oxford Street?

· *Something brisk and almost dangerous about these two young men.*

RICHARDS (*smiling at* SHARON). Oh yes, I think I knew this was here.

1ST YOUNG MAN. So where amongst all this rubbish is 2047?

   1ST YOUNG MAN *has stopped in front of shelves of film cans, he moves along, calling out numbers.*

2ND YOUNG MAN (*waving at cans of film*). It's mostly all of tanks – tank drivers taking their driving test!

1ST YOUNG MAN. 2041, 42, 2043. (*He stops.*) Oh yes – it's not here is it. (*He looks round.*) That's the load we were told to throw out, 2043 to 2049, I was thinking it sounded familiar that number.

SHARON. I thought they'd just been moved here!

2ND YOUNG MAN. Yeah, we got a message, day before yesterday. (*Giving shelf a venomous kick.*) I was pleased. At last we're going to be throwing out some of these rubbishy cans!

SHARON. How convenient.

RICHARDS. When did you throw it out?

1ST YOUNG MAN. Yesterday. Put them in black rubbish bags and chucked them out into the street.

   SHARON *immediately turns towards the exit.*

2ND YOUNG MAN. No point hurrying, the truck's just taken it away. (*Smile.*) We heard the noise. . .

RICHARDS. That's the end of that.

SHARON (*urgent*). Where would it have gone?

1ST YOUNG MAN (*grinning slightly*). The tip, where else. Of course, if you run, you might catch it!

Exterior: Tottenham Court Road Area – Day

A high shot of RICHARDS *and* SHARON *emerging into the bright light from the bunker above the deep tunnel, just off Tottenham Court Road.*

RICHARDS' *car has a parking ticket flapping on the windscreen.*

RICHARDS. If you're about to ask me where the main rubbish tip is, don't bother.

SHARON. I know what you're thinking – you're worrying about your work, feeling guilty. But it can wait a day, just today won't make any difference. (*Following his glance towards two city gents.*) Don't want to be seen with me do you? (*Her sudden, intense smile.*) Don't worry about that. Aren't you glad you've been down these tunnels?

RICHARDS. No.

A garbage truck rumbles down an adjoining street, they both see it.

SHARON *glances at the disappearing truck and then at* RICHARDS.

I am not following that truck.

SHARON (*staring straight at him*). Of course not.

Exterior: Rubbish Tip – Day

Wide shot of the massive rubbish tip on the edge of London, the line of garbage lorries queuing to unload, the squalls of seagulls overhead.

RICHARDS' *car gingerly driving to the edge of the tip, on the very edge of the frame, with the trucks moving all around them.*

We cut to RICHARDS *and* SHARON *moving along the paths that criss-cross the area – jumble of colour and a multitude of objects, the detritus of the city, household goods, the contents of whole rooms seem to have been disposed of together, even if in a squashed form.*

SHARON *moving ahead of him, bobbing and weaving round the objects.*

RICHARDS. This is stupid – there's no way anybody could find anything in this. . .

SHARON *far ahead of him, looking a startling presence in these surroundings, her red hair and her fur coat. She turns calling back to him.*

SHARON. Yes there is, we find out where the most recent arrivals have come in. . .

She is standing between two great mounds of rubbish.

You can leave me here if you like. . .

We cut to them going over the peak of the mound, below them one of the valleys of the tip, and in it they see various tramps scavenging on the side of one of the mountains of rubbish. A tramp looks up towards them.

RICHARDS (*indicating the tramps*). They probably think we've come to join them.

Cut to them moving fast along a trench between walls of rubbish, legs of a broken mannequin sticking out of the side – SHARON is holding forth as she moves in front of him, subjective shot from his point of view as he tries to keep up with her.

SHARON. Did you know the police, in their training school go and collect dead tramps, and they bury them, in Hendon, and let their bodies decompose, so young policemen can have practice in digging up bodies, so they get used to it.

RICHARDS. Another of your made-up facts Sharon!

SHARON *smiles back at him.*

As RICHARDS follows her, he keeps seeing things of interest, an ornamental candle-stick, some old books with white, ivory-coloured covers.

Oxfam ought to hold a jumble sale here.

He plucks one of the white books from the wall of the trench as they pass.

Good lord, this looks like, this may well be a first edition of a
Conan Doyle.

SHARON (*seeing this, calling back to him*). Glad you came now?

RICHARDS *picks up something else.*

RICHARDS. Somebody's school reports, I must have a look at
these.

*A white tape stretches across the mouth of the trench, they duck
underneath it.*

*They come out into the main section of the tip, the central mounds,
there is the sound of radios, walkie-talkies jabbering.*

*In the distance the police, and two men in suits, HILLCOMBE and
BOYCE, officials looking like civil servants, moving in front of the
police, poking at things as they move, seemingly looking for
something, the police keeping a respectable distance.*

(*Watching them.*) The whole world's here today.

*Officials moving very gingerly through rubbish. A gust of wind blows
some papers into SHARON and RICHARDS' faces, fluttering past
them, RICHARDS grabs some of them as they brush by, and
glances at them.*

(*Grins.*) Some records of something, or somebody . . . look like
medical records.

*He stuffs them into his pocket to join the book, as they move down
the slope.*

*Suddenly a face appears above them on one of the mounds – a
MAN of about 40, but with white hair and incredibly yellow teeth.*

YELLOW-TOOTHED MAN. What are you doing here? This
area is closed, this part of the park is closed today.

SHARON. Why?

YELLOW-TOOTHED MAN. Park's closed, come back another
day.

SHARON (*calling up at him*). Where would you find a delivery from central London, from around Tottenham Court Road, where would it have come. . .

YELLOW-TOOTHED MAN (*cutting her off*). Central London? You're mad if you think you'll find it here. No chance! It will have gone to the incinerator in Edmonton of course.

Looking down at her, as if everybody should know that.

(*Slight grin.*) Thrown something away you shouldn't have?

SHARON (*shouting back*). Yes.

YELLOW-TOOTHED MAN. If it went today, it's possible you may still have a chance. Always takes them a while to get around to burning – they burn slow there.

RICHARDS *and* SHARON *stare up at him.*

It may not have gone into the fire yet.

Exterior/Interior: Incinerator Complex – Day

Cut to RICHARDS *driving into the hard, modern, glass and concrete forecourt of the incinerator. A black limousine is parked incongruously among the garbage trucks.*

Cut to SHARON *and* RICHARDS *in the interior of the incinerator complex, the vaults outside the furnaces.*

They are moving along a catwalk and staring down into the great vats below them. It is like the inside of an enormous concrete tanker – a truly spectacular sight. It is given a peculiarly alluring quality by the diffused light that occurs because a cool spray of water is constantly playing on the rubbish, everything near the incinerator therefore is seen through a slight haze. A crane moves above the vats, with its scooper falling to pick up a load.

RICHARDS *is truly startled walking into this unexpected place, a* PUDGY MAN, *very well dressed is guiding them along the catwalk. His manner suggests he could just as easily be showing them over his nightclub.*

PUDGY MAN. This is my favourite view, good isn't it? (*Leaning*

over the side.) I never get tired of it. (*He grins.*) The magical
world of waste. (*Looking down.*) You got the innards of London
down there, every day of the year including Christmas day and
Good Friday, what more could you ask for! (*He moves along
catwalk.*) If it came in today, what you're looking for, it should
still be down there. . .

RICHARDS *looks down and sees two men in dark glasses carefully
putting their waste, documents, envelopes, a framed picture, by hand
into one of the vats, ready for the incinerator.*

RICHARDS. Who are those?

PUDGY MAN. The Poles of course . . . we get the Israelis too,
and the Americans all drive out from their embassies, make a
day trip of it. (*Reproachfully.*) Some people take a great deal of
trouble over their waste disposal, they take care, if it's
confidential or of a secret nature, they want to handle it
themselves, see it go into the fire personally.

RICHARDS (*staring down at the men*). I expect they look forward
to it.

PUDGY MAN (*watching the Poles*). I do anyway – I get a bottle of
Vodka from them each time.

SHARON *has moved along the catwalk ahead of them; she's
suddenly shouting and running down some stairs towards the vats.*

SHARON. I think I've seen it. Come on – there's just one can
down there.

PUDGY MAN *watching* SHARON *running down towards the
vats.*

PUDGY MAN. Must be something important.

RICHARDS (*half to himself*). Yes, or she's certifiable.

We cut to them, SHARON *and* RICHARDS *moving along the
second level, as the crane moves above them, towards the vats. The
two Poles in dark glasses watching them.*

SHARON. I think it is there . . . in the last one.

She's pointing to where the crane is picking up the rubbish, she has stumbled on the catwalk and is indicating he should get it.

RICHARDS. No way am I going to go in there.

He moves up to the vat, as the crane dangles above him.

There is one can of film visible among the general rubbish. He's about to walk away and leave it, when he sees shining out from the middle of the vat, just catching his eye, what looks very like the necklace that BARBARA threw away. He can't resist jumping over the side of the vat and picking it up. It is the same necklace. As he collects the necklace, he also picks up the film, which is covered in general gunge.

SHARON is staring down at him, over the side, as he stands in the middle of the vat.

SHARON (*slight smile*). Found something of yours have you? (*She stares at him.*) Made your trip worthwhile then.

Cut to SHARON standing on a platform high above the vats, using the spray from the water jets to wipe off the dirt from the number on the can. It is 2043 – the wrong can.

The wrong one, and the last one, they've burnt the rest.

She lets it go, and it falls down towards the vats.

Exterior: London Park – Day

We follow the falling film as it plunges the 100 feet down towards the incinerator but just before it hits the bottom, we cut to a sunbaked evening, a gently rolling shot, a track with RICHARDS and SHARON down a broad walk in a park lined with trees, with a white Regency house staring down at us at the end of the path, and a large pond. A totally English scene, an autumn bonfire gently smouldering in the distance.

SHARON *and* RICHARDS *walking slightly apart but parallel,* RICHARDS *is still holding the book he found,* SHARON *moving in and out of the trees. They are both eating water melons. Sudden sense of refreshment, of coming up for air.*

SHARON (*brushing her coat, as she moves, calling over to him*). Do you think this smell will ever come off?

RICHARDS. What smell?

SHARON. The smell from all that rubbish, the gunge – it's on
you too you know.

RICHARDS (*staring at* SHARON). Why you so interested in all
this Sharon?

Indicating the package, her film she's still carrying.

You really believe there's some sort of mystery inside there?

SHARON. Yes. I wondered when you'd start wanting reasons.

Her piercing smile, she is moving slightly ahead of him on the path.

Because I'm curious. (*Looking back at him down the path.*) Isn't
that a good enough reason? Can I see your book by the way?

*He moves slightly nearer her as he gives her the first edition to look
at he found on the tip.*

And what exactly is *your* work then? What's it for? All these
years of research?

RICHARDS *surprised.*

You didn't think I'd ask did you?

RICHARDS (*watching her as they walk*). It's an investigation . . .
into educational methods . . . the way we teach, and into the
way children see things. And I mean literally see things.

SHARON *moves just slightly ahead of him along the path, he's
watching her red hair.*

I'm testing the theory that kids, now no longer can retain
information from the printed page, that we should accept the
influence of television and the image, rather than fight it – and
use it as the *main* instrument in the classrooms, staring out of
the wall at you. (*Slight smile.*) In a sentence – throw the books
out of school; fill it with screens. Even literature can be taught
like that up to a point, all history certainly.

SHARON *ahead of him on the path.*

Because no one under 18 can concentrate – unless the image moves. And then only in 5 minute segments, before they need some commercials. (*Watching her seemingly not attending to him, he smiles at her*). As you are proving at this very moment by not listening to a word I'm saying.

He sees she's watching very closely some people coming towards them along the path – two men in sports jackets and flannels as if they've been to Henley or the Derby, with a girl walking between them dressed in very expensive clothes. One of the men is walking a small dog. SHARON watching them with a sudden interest, a suspicious slightly paranoid look, as if she thinks they are watching her, which RICHARDS notices.

Suddenly she snaps out of it and looks straight at him as if she's been listening to everything.

SHARON. So you know what you're going to end up proving in the book – even though you haven't finished the research.

RICHARDS (*surprised by this – he smiles*). Possibly . . .

SHARON (*staring straight at him*). See, I knew it! That's why you're here . . . I may or may not be an interesting case history.

RICHARDS. No you don't fit, wrong age group.

SHARON (*turning on the path, slightly ahead of him*). How old do you think I am?

RICHARDS. Seventeen and a half, maybe a month off 18.

SHARON (*giving no indication if he's right or not*). You like figures don't you, percentages and statistics and all that, thirty seven and a half per cent thinks this . . . five out of seven people sleep in pyjamas, that sort of thing.

RICHARDS. Yes, that's what I am. A statistician (*he smiles*) of a rather classy kind. There's something very safe about figures, very satisfying when you arrive at a statistic, a precise percentage, because so much effort, such an enormous amount of work goes into it, and the result is very simple, very short, and nobody is in a position to contradict it.

He sees SHARON is again suddenly in a world of her own, they have gone round the edge of the pond and suddenly there are the three people in sports jackets and flannels and with the dog walking in front of them again.

SHARON. Do you think there's something odd about those people? (*She's looking at the young man with the dog.*) He's been watching us I think . . .

He follows her gaze, her paranoid look towards the young man with the dog, we see him thinking – this girl really is a little crazy.

SHARON *suddenly moves away from him as the group of three come nearer and nearer to them.*

I have to go – I have to go *now.*

She runs off down the path, still holding his book. Before she disappears she calls back.

You never know I may need your help again.

Interior: RICHARDS' *Lounge – Evening*

The light is just going, the main room in RICHARDS' *house, the telephone answering machine in the foreground of the shot, with its red light on,* RICHARDS' *shape just discernible, stretched out in back of shot absolutely exhausted, oblivious of everything.*

The machine clicks on, and begins to tape . . . and we hear the voice calling as if we were the machine listening, RICHARDS *doesn't move.*

WOMAN'S VOICE (*formal, like a secretary*). Hello . . . this is Janet, Mr. Richards . . . I'm not sure where you are. Are you all right? You don't seem to have kept any of your appointments today, I hope nothing has happened, please ring me at home if you feel like it. I hope to see you tomorrow as normal. So . . . I mean, goodbye.

Exterior: A Gravel Drive – Day

We cut into a subjective shot, outside, down a gravel path, with a late fifties car parked at the side. The film stock is different – the visual quality not as clear, or immediate.

Exterior: School Grounds – Day

A SCHOOLMASTER *is approaching, a seemingly very tall figure, sweeping towards a* SMALL BOY *of about eleven, down the gravel path. The* BOY *is dressed in school uniform. The* MASTER *bears down on him and is almost past him, when he shouts.*

SCHOOLMASTER. RICHARDS!

The SMALL BOY *freezes.*

Come here! Wondering what marks you got aren't you.

SMALL BOY. No sir, not really sir. . .

SCHOOLMASTER. I'm not going to tell you.

Suddenly hitting him over the head with an exercise book; though as he is hitting the BOY, *he is praising him at the same time.*

You're a bright little chap! (*Hits him with book.*) One of the best . . . I'd say one of the cleverest blighters we've had here recently . . . but he doesn't make the most of it. (*Hits him with book.*) What don't you do?

SMALL BOY. Don't make the most of it sir . . .

SCHOOLMASTER (*looking down at him, continuing to hit him*). A clever shrimp. A surprisingly clever little shrimp. A pity he wastes it! Why doesn't he fulfil his potential! I wonder why?

He sweeps on with his back to the BOY *as he shouts out.*

(*Holding exercise book above his head as he sweeps away.*) You want to know what I've written in this don't you? You shouldn't be so eager to find out.

SCHOOLMASTER *tosses the book into a litter bin incongruously placed in the centre of the path. As he sweeps away, the* BOY *notices the* MASTER *has bare feet.*

Disjointed immediate cut, as in dreams. An Armstrong Siddley car standing at the end of gravel drive. SMALL BOY *and* SECOND BOY *standing in school uniforms staring up at it, moving round it, touching it, its doors are open, leather seats glistening, 50's music playing from the car radio.*

SMALL BOY. If I could get better marks I would get in to this car and really drive it.

SECOND BOY (*touching the car*). Drive and drive!

SMALL BOY. Yes go on safari, go across the deserts, right across the world, go on the most incredible journey ever planned. But I *never* get good enough marks!

50's music playing.

SECOND BOY *takes paper flapping out of the radiator grill of the car.*

SECOND BOY. Here's your report, see. (*He plucks it out of radiator.*) Maybe you shouldn't look at it!

SMALL BOY *turns pages of report but the remarks are all runny inside like soap.*

50's music playing on soundtrack.

Limbo SHARON's face

Suddenly SHARON's face appears in large close-up, staring straight, the warm smile, then the haunted look.

Interior: RICHARDS' Lounge – Day

RICHARDS' *waking still on the sofa, crumpled up, still wearing all his clothes. He glances at his jacket sleeve, a small brightly coloured beetle, acquired at the rubbish tip or the incinerator is climbing up his sleeve.*

Exterior: River and Barge – Day

A shot of the river with sound or things being thrown out of a window down into a rubbish barge, and

Interior: Office and Corridor – Day

then a shot down a dark passage, with the light of an office at the end of it, and a MIDDLE-AGED WOMAN, who we can't see saying

'No, all of that goes cut, we're throwing *all* of that out, just keep every third number. I don't want to have to say that again.'

Exterior: London Back Street – Day

Cut to SHARON moving along a back street, very few people around, she's moving fast, and glancing over her shoulder, glancing suspiciously at a MAN standing at the mouth of the alleyway that she is moving down.

Exterior: London Street – Day

We cut to RICHARDS moving down the street, past the mansion flats, as when he was grabbed by SHARON. As he gets level with the doorway he approaches gingerly and steers very wide of it, so there's no chance of it happening again. There's nobody in the doorway.

He rounds the corner. In the next shot, he walks slap into the stomach of somebody.

When he looks who it is, he is astonished to see it is his old SCHOOLMASTER who we saw in the dream.

SCHOOLMASTER (*furious*). Mind where you are going for goodness sake.

RICHARDS. Good God – Mr. Jackson? It's you isn't it?

SCHOOLMASTER (*impatient*). Yes, and who are you?

RICHARDS. James Richards.

SCHOOLMASTER. No you're not. (*Studying him.*) Oh yes – now I look at you, you probably are. Just a little neater than usual.

We cut to them further on down the street. RICHARDS can't take his eyes off the SCHOOLMASTER, who looks smaller than in the dream, but hardly any older, just a few touches of grey.

(*Who is carrying a heavy bag of books.*) You couldn't carry this could you? Have to get out of this infernal city before it drives me mad, a day trip is about all I can stand, damned ugly place isn't it. (*Suddenly to RICHARDS.*) You still live here I suppose.

RICHARDS. Yes, I do.

SCHOOLMASTER *shakes his head sorrowfully.*

SCHOOLMASTER. Are you married or not, I've lost count.

RICHARDS. I've only been married *once.*

SCHOOLMASTER. Once too often. (*Tone suddenly changes.*) You haven't got any loose change have you I could borrow. I've only got five pound notes; I hate waiting for change, always trying to short change in London aren't they? (*He looks at* RICHARDS.) I'll send you a postal order – or a book token.

RICHARDS *starts looking for the change. He is already holding the books. He is fighting hard the instinctive desire to treat this ridiculous man with schoolboy respect.*

(*Watching* RICHARDS *searching for the money.*) So still keeping this writing thing going are you? What do you do all day? My God if I could have your spare time! You ought to be able to produce ten books a year on that. (*Counting the loose change.*) I read your book in fact, now I come to think of it, interesting theme, poor construction – the chapters were in the wrong order.

Suddenly he seems more formidable, more serious. RICHARDS *behaving like a small boy.*

Could have been an excellent book, instead of merely mildly informative. Threw away a chance there I think. (*He puts change away.*) So when is the next one due? You certainly haven't got any quicker have you! (*Looks at him.*) It'll be an improvement no doubt, the next one.

Suddenly stops, RICHARDS *watching him fascinated.*

By the way, you couldn't be so kind and just go and look for a taxi for me, I'm running a little short of time.

Interior: Office – Day

The room by the river we saw in long shot before, with the middle-aged woman's voice. Now we see her a hard faced impassive looking MIDDLE-AGED WOMAN, *but very smartly dressed. She is sitting at a formica desk. We can see the river behind her through a window, which has security bars on it.* SHARON *is standing at the other end of the room, through an open door we can see in darkness a large storage room.*

MIDDLE AGED WOMAN (*moving papers on her desk, her tone icily polite*). I am going to count to ten, and when I have reached that number, and if you're still here, I will call the police.

Pause. They stare at each other.

SHARON. I have just found out about this place – on the grapevine – that this is where a lot of old film is being delivered, film that was classified as secret. (*Pause.*) Are you just a secretary or is it you that's in charge? All I need to do is have a look.

MIDDLE AGED WOMAN. I can't tell you that.

SHARON (*glancing at empty office beyond*). It must get lonely here! And you've been given a budget to transfer exactly one third of it onto video, isn't that right?

MIDDLE AGED WOMAN. I can't tell you that either. I'm neither confirming nor denying that. And I'm still counting. . .

SHARON. And all I want to see is if my film was put on video before you chucked it out, that's all!

MIDDLE AGED WOMAN. I can't let that happen.

SHARON. It's very innocent, it's called 'The Hedgerows of England'. I'm working for a very important writer, Mr. James Richards who you will of course have heard of . . . he has friends all over Whitehall . . . I have a note here to prove it. (*Threatening smile.*) It might not be such a dumb idea to co-operate with me.

MIDDLE AGED WOMAN *glancing at the note* SHARON *took from* RICHARDS.

SHARON *moving up and down, a febrile presence, something formidable in her single-mindedness.*

How do you choose the films to be chucked out anyway? Stick pins in a list? (*Mimicking her.*) I'll have that one please. Or is it every third number, 3, 6, 173.

MIDDLE AGED WOMAN. I have my own methods which seem to be giving satisfaction.

SHARON. I bet they are. I'm going in there.

She goes to the door, MIDDLE-AGED WOMAN *suddenly like lightning jumps up.*

MIDDLE AGED WOMAN. *NO!*

She has really shouted as if her life depended on it.

SHARON *and she face each other.*

Come away from that door!

SHARON. I'm not leaving here till I've seen in there – We'll see who gives first! (*She advances up to desk.*) My money's on me, usually is. Have you reached ten yet, or is that confidential as well?

Interior: RICHARDS' *Lounge – Day*

RICHARDS' *house, main room, Saturday afternoon, atmosphere comfortable, drinks, dappled afternoon light, shadows playing on the walls, cool interior,* ANTHONY *sitting on the pastel coloured sofa with a* DARK-HAIRED WOMAN, *looking very similar in dress and demeanour to the one in the dinner party scene, but with different coloured hair, we get the impression he can't keep a relationship going for more than a few weeks.*

ANTHONY (*leaning back, dangling his arm over the edge of the sofa*). And he made you carry his books!

RICHARDS. Yes.

ANTHONY. I'd like to have seen that, you scurrying behind your old teacher!

RICHARDS. It's extraordinary how teachers don't age, isn't it, must be 27 years ago since he taught me, if anything he'd got younger. Smaller of course, your old teachers always shrink, but he looked ridiculously young. (*Pouring drink.*) And a meeting like that jangles all sorts of things inside, pieces of the past, things you'd forgotten.

ANTHONY. And he just popped up in the street! (*He smiles.*) What are the chances of that happening, the percentage, the day after you dreamed about him?

RICHARDS' *sharp smile. The phone starts ringing, small high pitched ring,* RICHARDS *makes no attempt to answer it.*

How's the work? (*Turning to the dark haired girl.*) You must remind me to explain to you how James spends the day!

RICHARDS *watching the phone out of the corner of his eye.*

RICHARDS. I'm going away in the next 48 hours, probably tomorrow. I've finally decided where.

ANTHONY. You have!

RICHARDS (*slight smile*). But I don't think I'm telling anyone.

DARK HAIRED WOMAN *gives* RICHARDS *an alarmingly shrewd stare seemingly detecting his restless state.*

DARK HAIRED WOMAN. When you're tired of London – you're tired of life. Didn't somebody say that (*she looks around*) that horrible man Dr. Johnson.

They have all been pretending to ignore the fact the phone is ringing.

ANTHONY. Answer the fucking phone, please James.

RICHARDS *picks up phone, acting very casually.*

SHARON'S VOICE. You have to come . . . (*louder*) you have to come *now.*

RICHARDS. I can't, I'm busy.

SHARON. You have to come, I've found it.

RICHARDS. I'll think about it. *OK.*

Puts down phone – they're looking at him.

Interior: Video Factory – Night

The warren-like building, the video reproducing firm, the smoky, dark, atmosphere . . . a party is being held. Halloween. There are not many guests among the machines, but the young workforce of the place, plus the older mid-European receptionist are dressed up for the party.

A lot of drink and food spread around the place, balancing on the top of machines, crab salads, whole fish with their mouths decorated shining among the shelves of stored tape, and a surprising amount of flowers and Halloween decorations, giving the banks of machines an exotic look. An atmosphere of fashionable young things, men and women, intimidating, slightly glacial, music pounding.

A subjective camera movement draws RICHARDS *in, as he moves along the warren-like passages. Staring at the party guests, spots of lights among the underlit darkness, and some of the screens are playing, various fragments of video flickering out, current Schlock movies, advertisements, pop promos . . . and in the corner a television picking up by satellite a wavy signal of Russian television.*

RICHARDS *is beautifully dressed, elegant, immaculate, he moves along this world as a detached observer. But throughout the scene, he is drinking, casually refuelling, not realizing quite how much is going down.*

CURTIS, *the boy in the long coat and wearing spectacles is gobbling food down in the foreground, scooping it up in great handfuls.*

CURTIS. You have to eat it quickly or Brewster takes it away. He always ends his parties at one o'clock, he's worried about losing valuable working time. He pulls the plugs at one o'clock. So eat it quickly before he locks the food up again.

RICHARDS *watching* BREWSTER *across the room in his luminous spectacles.*

RICHARDS. He makes everyone go home.

CURTIS. Word hard and play hard, that's what he likes to see happen here.

He pulls the fish in half, starts eating it, points to SHARON *in the distance.*

She's put you to work has she – 'The mystery in a film' – she used to go on at me about it, how she HAD to find it. She hasn't got many friends you know. (*Peers at* RICHARDS.) You've been crawling about in tunnels I hear. (*Looking towards* SHARON.) She is probably crazy isn't she? But it's fun all the same, I wish I had the time to help her.

RICHARDS *moves on, deeper into the warren, a group of the* YOUNG PARTY GUESTS *are standing around the television set showing Russian programmes. They are calling out remarks at it, some of them roaring with laughter.*

Drop a bomb on Russia!

Look at secret police on the set, yeah the one wearing antlers, he's the K.G.B. in disguise . . .

Send her to Siberia.

Stock Shot: Nazi Footage

Others standing by a video nasty, which we see is a film involving people in Nazi uniforms. One of the kids is sitting on a stool opposite, eating peanuts from a large bowl, like gobbling popcorn, and at periodic intervals saying:

Heil Hitler . . . yeah hack that bit off you gormless shit, heil Hitler.

His tone is matter of fact as he does this, and we cannot tell if he's trying to be funny or not.

We see RICHARDS *taking in their ignorance, watching them, an objective stare.*

Stock Shot: Demolition Derby Footage

A really beautiful girl is leaning against a machine as a violent smash-up of cars, a demolition derby, is taking place behind her on video, as she delicately eats a celery dip.

A young couple are locked together, kissing, wrapped round each other, squashed into a crevice between two video machines.

In the middle of all this, the party with video playing, SHARON *beckons to* RICHARDS, *out of the shadows at the far end of the room.*

He is taken by surprise because she is dressed in a striking fashionable dress, and looks older, more sophisticated, for a moment he doesn't recognize her. SHARON gives him a warm smile of greeting and he smiles back in surprise.

SHARON. What are you gawping at?

RICHARDS. You look completely different each time I see you!

SHARON (*smiles*). You don't! (*Her mood darkens.*) Come here, quickly. There's a problem (*as he moves with her*) a terrible problem.

RICHARDS. What?

For a moment he thinks she means something really serious.

SHARON. There's something wrong with the tape. (*Excitedly, we can hardly hear what she's saying.*) I was right, the film had been transferred onto video. It's all here. (*She indicates monitor screen.*) But it's *dark*. Something wrong with the quality, it's too dark.

She switches V.H.S. machine on tape running, the screen flickering into life.

But I think you can just see . . . almost, just.

SHARON *stares at the screen.*

Watch.

But it is SHARON RICHARDS watches, she has taken a large toy watch out of her pocket, and a small furry animal, as she moves in front of the screen. Suddenly contradicting the sophisticated image she had seemingly been projecting.

As RICHARDS watches her flick the toy watch, even wind it up, he realises again that this girl is more than a little strange.

SHARON (*pointing*). Look.

The video screen is completely black. CURTIS is also there, standing, craning to see anything on the dark screen.

You can just see a face, her face I think, *you* can lighten the tape. We've already worked on this piece you see.

Interior: Court Room – Day

She's pointing at the black screen, we move in close, we can just make out a woman's face moving in a room, and three dark faces, shadowy almost, sitting at a table, they are like figures in a negative, we can only just make them out, they are no more than shadows.

RICHARDS *is totally unimpressed.*

RICHARDS. Great camera work (*sharp smile*) appropriate film for Halloween . . . Just a lot of old shadows.

CURTIS (watching). I can almost make something out.

SHARON. Watch.

B/W Caption

She has put a movement into slow motion on V.H.S. a face moving, maybe a woman crying but it is ridiculously dark. The black tape runs to its end, SHARON staring intently, only the last moments are clear, a caption saying 'See also Hop-Pickers in Kent!' complete with the slightly surprising exclamation mark.

SHARON. We have to find that one.

RICHARDS *moves away from SHARON as she rewinds the tape to look at it again, her possessed manner, she looks to him a comical figure for a moment, swinging her toy watch, watching a completely dark picture with rapt interest. But then she darts a look towards him as he moves away, a strongly attractive, dangerously animated look. It is the contrast that intrigues him.*

Exterior: Street – Night

We cut to the PARTYGOERS moving outside into the night, some excited, expectant, some bored, people are calling 'Come on it's starting . . . come on . . . '

On the house opposite, set up specially for the party, is a display of Housewatch, the projection of six different film images in the six separate windows of the house, filling up its whole facade, a giant cat scrambling to get out of one window, a woman screaming out of another, fire and animals and children staring. An effect of startling, extraordinary force. These disjointed images playing in the windows of an ordinary London house.

RICHARDS *stares at these dislocated images and at the young people standing below the house, drunk, kissing, or watching, glacially separate coolly smoking.* RICHARDS *watches* SHARON *appear by his side, give him a momentary intense smile and then move off winding her toy watch talking to herself.* RICHARDS *takes another drink from a bottle.* BREWSTER, *the boss of the place appears by his side.*

BREWSTER. You liked the show?

RICHARDS *nods gently staring up at the house.*

I tell you one thing, I always *think* at parties, start to worry. Most of the time I'm too busy to worry, but at parties I have the most terrible time, start examining my whole life.

RICHARDS. Is that a good idea!

BREWSTER. Certainly not. (*Waving his hand at the machines.*) There have been some frightening moments recently when business has gone far too quiet, a firm like this opens every day of the week, a new one pops up. (*He waves at the screens.*) We will copy anything anybody wants. We cater for some funny tastes I can tell you, got asked the other day for 50 copies of a tape about ears being syringed. (*He laughs to himself.*) To each their own! It takes people's minds off things. . .

RICHARDS (*staring up at the house*). Of course.

BREWSTER (*his luminous spectacles shining*). Come on, come with me, we grown ups belong inside.

Interior: Video Factory – Night

We cut to BREWSTER *and* RICHARDS *with drink in front of them.* BREWSTER *is sitting with his back to four televisions, which are showing a girl in a bikini riding a killer whale round a pool.*

BREWSTER. I think on fast forward now you know, suddenly watching the news, and desperate to put it on fast forward, but I can't because it's going out live! I don't think I've seen a film

all the way through for the last three years. I feel acutely
depressed if I see an ending – I prefer everything to be cut off in
the middle. I can't bear a sense of completeness. (*Staring at*
RICHARDS *through his spectacles.*) Do you always drink as
much as this?

RICHARDS (*casual smile*). No, I haven't done this for years.

*The lighting and camera angle have imperceptibly changed,
heightened.*

BREWSTER. I'm suffering from one particularly agonizing
complaint at the moment, I am having the most extraordinarily
vivid dreams this year, but I can't remember a single moment
of them, not a single frame of them. I just wake with this
sensation – they were extraordinary but they have vanished.
Before I could always remember at least one in three, it's a
form of modern torture knowing they are getting better and
better, but I can't hold them in my head.

BREWSTER *moves.*

So I have started putting them on tape . . . I have all my
dreams on video tape, they record automatically as I sleep.

RICHARDS (*answering him perfectly naturally*). You've managed
that? I've always wondered about that, wanted to do it. . .

BREWSTER (*by a V.H.S. machine – indicating his collection*). Why
is it impossible to *tell* people your dreams? One's always bored
stiff by other people's dreams, you become so impatient with the
illogical sequence of events. But if you can show them, like
home movies, people can cope slightly more.

RICHARDS. I have a recurring dream of having buried
something locked up in an old car.

BREWSTER (*stretching forward and plucking a tape out*). Yes, I've
got it here somewhere.

He pushes it into the V.H.S. machine, images from RICHARDS'
dream appear on the screen.

RICHARDS (*getting up, moving over to screen to watch*). This is one
of *my* dreams – I don't know how you could have got hold of it.

Exterior: A Driveway – Day

We see the TWO SMALL BOYS *sitting in the Armstrong Siddley staring through the windscreen, the engine on, the radio on.*

SMALL BOY (*at steering wheel*). It's in the boot. I don't know why I hid it there. I can't get it out now.

SECOND BOY. But we can't start until you get it out.

RICHARDS (*standing inspecting tape*). Yes this is the bit, very obviously a guilt dream. Rather worryingly banal in fact.

We see the TWO LITTLE BOYS *trying to open the boot of the car.*

SMALL BOY. It's locked. I told you I can't get it open. It'll smell won't it soon.

He runs his finger along the side of the boot. Black sand beginning to come through the crack.

Interior: School Study – Day

The image fills the screen, the same SCHOOLMASTER *sitting at a desk, a jam jar with a large water beetle in the foreground,* MASTER'*s legs up on desk.*

SCHOOLMASTER. You're leaving here today, and you still haven't done anything like what I expected. You've done well, but nothing spectacular. You're nearly 40 now . . . I've lost your report.

RICHARDS (*watching*). Yes, this the bit about doing better – (*looking at* MASTER) stupid old twit, turn the volume down. The business about me sheltering behind facts, immersing myself in statistics instead of being a more creative thinker, locking things away inside and refusing to use them. I know it by heart. (*Loud at screen.*) But I haven't got the energy! Don't you understand. . .

Exterior: A Driveway – Day

1ST SMALL BOY (*looking through the windscreen*). We'll never get there now, we never will.

Limbo: SHARON's *Face*

SHARON's *face appears, the sense of* RICHARDS *watching, and the images on the small screen have ellided, he's slipped into them.*

SHARON's *hand is undoing his shirt and pulling it off.*

SHARON (*tugging*). Come on, come on.

> *She turns, in a T-shirt, sweat running down her neck, her hair matted, touching him, then we see her sitting at a table laying out postcards of London in a fan-shaped pattern. Postcards of Beefeaters, Big Ben, of a lurid sunset over St. Paul's.*

> *The picture begins to darken, darkening all the time.*

Limbo: BARBARA's *Face*

BARBARA, *his wife appears.*

RICHARDS. I've been meaning to tell you for a long time. I don't know why I didn't tell you. (*Quiet.*) I do love you still. (*Her face fading.*) Why's your face darkening Barbara?

> *There is a shot of* BREWSTER *standing by his side watching the screen too.*

You're right it is better to show people. How much would it cost me to take this home.

BREWSTER. This tape of your dream? £10 for two days, £20 every day you're over that.

RICHARDS (*quiet*). Do I have to pay a deposit as well?

Exterior: A Park – Day

He is suddenly walking beside SHARON *down a broad path, she is pulling his shirt free of him, as he moves.*

SHARON. You've been here before of course.

RICHARDS. Of course.

SHARON. I don't believe you.

RICHARDS. I know this city backwards. It's my native city.

SHARON (*turning challenging, her face really close to him*). Just
  because it's your native city – doesn't mean you know it.

Interior: Tunnel (Tottenham Court Road) – Day

*Subjective shot travelling through the tunnels under Tottenham Court
Road.*

Exterior: A Park – Day

Cut back to RICHARDS *walking with* SHARON.

RICHARDS. Oh yes it does! And it's finished this place. Just
  living off tourists . . . (*looking at* SHARON) and pop videos.

SHARON. You *really* think you know this city do you!

  Sudden blackness, we hear RICHARDS' *voice in a frightened
  whisper, he can only see shadows.*

RICHARDS. Why can't I see anything? Why's it so dark
  suddenly?

Interior: SHARON's *Flat – Day*

RICHARDS *wakes with a start, his eyes flashing open from the
dream, to a brilliantly sunny, white empty room.*

*A really hot white light, the room has crumbling plaster, peeling paint,
high ceiling, a large full length mirror propped against the wall.*

From somewhere in the building there is distant music.

RICHARDS *at first thinks he is quite alone, looking down at himself,
he is lying on a narrow bed in a corner of the room, he sees he has been
half-undressed.*

*Everywhere across the floor of the room there is a mess. The drawers
have been pulled out. There is absolute chaos over the floor.*

RICHARDS *looks about the room, he's surprised to see in a corner a
model, home-made out of cardboard but brightly painted, of Piccadilly
Circus with the Masonic Temples underneath Regent Street, and toy
figures worshipping in the Temples dressed in their black robes.*

From an adjoining door he suddenly becomes aware of a rhythmic clanging noise. He moves across the room and pushes open the door.

In the mid-morning sun. SHARON *is sitting in a large old bath, with a one-year-old child with her in the water,* JODIE. *The child is banging joyfully on the side of the bath.* SHARON *looks up at him.*

SHARON (*pleasantly*). It's normal to knock you know. Go out and try again.

RICHARDS. Where am I?

SHARON. Where do you think, in my flat.

RICHARDS. Who's the child?

SHARON *staring straight at him.*

SHARON. My daughter.

RICHARDS *looking from* SHARON *to the small girl in the bath.*

We cut to SHARON *dressing, just buttoning up a very fashionable strikingly attractive dress. Looking at herself in the full length, cracked mirror.*

Throughout this sequence SHARON *is doing her hair, her lips, putting on tights, and shoes, gradually appearing more and more stunning, surprisingly fashionably and expensively dressed. Her appearance in striking contrast to the mess all over the floor.*

The child is sitting playing with the large toy watch and furry toy in the corner, the ones RICHARDS *saw* SHARON *holding in the scene before.*

RICHARDS. How could you possibly have a daughter. I mean where has she been all this time, where was she last night?

SHARON. At my mum's. I've just collected her. (*Piercing look.*) Where's the mystery?

RICHARDS. Hold old are you?

Sound of garbage truck moving down the street.

SHARON. You've already told me how old I am remember.

RICHARDS *glancing around the chaotic mess in the room startled to see a copy of his own book 'INSTEAD OF SEX?' with a bookmarker carefully placed showing how far SHARON has got. He looks at her but she has her back to him making herself up in the mirror.*

RICHARDS. What is this place, a squat or something? (*He moves around.*) I've been having the most ridiculous dreams. There *was* a party last night, wasn't there?

SHARON. Yes, of course. And you drank far too much and started snoring.

SHARON beginning to put on her coloured tights. Something extraordinarily assured about her manner.

Do you like the mess?

RICHARDS. Like it, what do you mean?

SHARON (*staring at him*). You think I did this, this is how you think I live?

RICHARDS. Yes.

SHARON not taking her eyes off him.

SHARON. Somebody did over the flat last night, while I was at the party. It's been *searched*, every inch . . . (*indicating marks*) they seem to have kicked the walls in frustration, (*sharp look*) they obviously didn't find anything!

RICHARDS. Don't start that please, it's too early in the morning for your paranoia. (*Sharp smile.*) Don't try to tell me your natural slovenliness is because MI5 has been crawling over your flat.

SHARON (*ignoring this*). They were looking for the film obviously. I left it hidden at the party, they'll never find it amongst all that other celluloid.

RICHARDS. For God's sake Sharon, stop this silly game, it isn't particularly funny any more. (*Snaps.*) Where are the rest of my clothes?

SHARON (*formidable*). Don't use that tone with me. Who got you home from the party last night anyway?

RICHARDS (*steely*). For that I'm grateful.

Turning over the mess with his foot, looking for his clothes.

Where is the book by the way, that first edition I found?

SHARON. That mouldy thing – I threw it out. It had beetles crawling out of it.

RICHARDS. You threw it out?

SHARON. Yes.

RICHARDS (*very sharp*). That's a brilliant move isn't it. That book was quite a find – the only thing of *interest* we have found and you throw it out!

RICHARDS suddenly furious, not being able to find his clothes, the dusty room and SHARON's attitude.

SHARON. What does one old book matter?

RICHARDS (*very sharp*). The *idea* that *you're* interested in the past. I don't know why I ever considered you might be. All this nonsense, this mystery about this film, it's just a puerile obsession, I mean even if you were right, if you bother to think it through, the very 'best' you could hope for is some flickering old film of somebody being clubbed to death and raped in an alleyway – that's the *best*.

SHARON. I don't want that – I'm not looking for shock horror. I'm just curious.

RICHARDS. It's a schoolgirl notion of what's interesting, just lazy thinking. . .

SHARON. Oh really! (*Fiery.*) And who's the one who knows the result of his research before he even started doing it! Because he knew the answer he needed to make him some money? Make his book sell! (*Loud.*) Who's the person who knows the answer to *everything*, even before it's asked. Who's smug enough to think. . .

RICHARDS (*cutting her off*). You're so ignorant Sharon. It amazes me.

He moves.

I can tell you that party last night was one of the most grisly evenings I've had recently, those kids there, all of you, completely oblivious to everything.

SHARON (*brushing her red hair vigorously as she faces him*). Yes, I saw you peering at everybody, voyeuristically taking notes – you looked so ridiculous. (*To* JODIE.) Don't you think there must be something funny about a person that spends all his time chatting up 'the young'. (*To* RICHARDS.) Any you, – the genius who knows everything – can't even tell when a room's been searched!

RICHARDS. I told you to stop that.

SHARON. You can tell me as many times as you like – you're not my father, (*pointing at* JODIE) or her father. (*Dangerous look.*) And don't ask! – you'd really like to know wouldn't you!

She moves, putting on her coat, she looks splendid.

Now I have to go out, try and find a new way of earning my living because of you. (*She moves.*) I'll be back at three. You can look after her till then. (*Indicating the child,* JODIE.)

RICHARDS (*amazed*). Look after her! (*He raises his voice.*) I have an appointment, what the hell do you mean!

SHARON *moving across the room.*

SHARON. She won't need feeding till I'm back. Just stay with her and keep her entertained. (*Pointing.*) Those are the toys, she'll teach you how to use them. Don't let her out of your sight – and be careful when you answer the door.

RICHARDS (*trying all his authority*). Sharon – come back here at once.

SHARON. Her name's Jodie, and like her mum, she prefers to be treated with some respect.

RICHARDS *runs out onto the peeling staircase after* SHARON *and yells after her as she descends.*

RICHARDS. Sharon – don't be ridiculous. You're not *allowed* to do this, come back here this instant.

SHARON *disappearing, her red hair bobbing into the darkness.*

RICHARDS *starting after her down the old staircase shouting after her:*

Is there such a thing as a phone in this place?

SHARON *disappearing.*

Can you just stop long enough to tell me that!

SHARON *at bottom of stairs, not looking back.*

And where's my car? What have you done with my car?

Shot of JODIE in doorway, she can just about stand, staring suspiciously at him. Their eyes meet.

Exterior: SHARON's Flat and Street – Day

Cut to RICHARDS in the pouring rain, trying to open his car door – as he holds JODIE in one arm, on his shoulder she is dangling one of her toys, and lets it drop into the rain and the mud, as he struggles to get the door open, RICHARDS sits her on the bonnet of the car, holding a plastic bag above her head, to shield her from the rain, as he scrabbles about for the rattle she's dropped.

RICHARDS (*to JODIE on the bonnet*). Behave yourself please – (*as she throws another toy from the bonnet*) make allowances for the inexperience. (*He smiles.*) You know, make an exception.

Interior of car. Shot of RICHARDS, without child seat, trying to fasten JODIE to the seat, with seat belt, she slips out underneath it onto the floor.

As he pulls her up, he notices through the rain-spattered windscreen a bald fat man watching from another car. RICHARDS takes it he's amused by his incompetence, wrestling with the child and the seat belt.

JODIE *throws the car keys out into the rain.*

Interior: Hairdressing Salon – Day

Cut to the foyer of a hairdressing salon, beautiful young things wafting around, spectacular hair styles, SHARON is queuing for a job as a receptionist in a line of other girls. While the other girls standing looking glacial, SHARON is moving restlessly all the time, looking about her, alert, never keeping still. A woman is handing out a form to all the girls waiting.

SHARON (*as she gets the form looking at all the questions*). Jesus – you would think they were trying to find a nuclear scientist instead of somebody to answer the bloody phones. (*Reading off form.*) Have I more than three 'A' levels?

The faces of the girls and boys already working in the salon, reflecting in the mirror opposite, covered in make up and hair colour, peacock eighties faces, and SHARON catches sight of herself, febrile, busy, suspicious.

Interior: The Cafe – Day

Cut to JODIE's face with streaks of raspberry ice cream over it.

In a wide shot we see we are in the same grand ornate but shabby room housing a cafeteria, that RICHARDS met SHARON in earlier in the film. Tramps still sheltering in the shadows with one cup of tea.

BARBARA is sitting opposite RICHARDS in the smoky light, the heavy rain is beating down clouding the window. BARBARA, coat still wet, though her hair is dry, she's looking very smart and contained. RICHARDS' clothes and hair wet.

BARBARA. James I've had to wait for you in this *awful* place.

People spitting and coughing behind her.

So you're going to tell me where you found this child. . . (*pause, looking at him*) with no mucking about, understand.

RICHARDS. I didn't find her – she was given to me.

RICHARDS sees a younger bag woman in the corner, muttering to herself, for a moment he's reminded of SHARON.

BARBARA (*sharp*). I told you – just give me a straight answer.

RICHARDS (*focusing on* BARBARA). It's this completely nutty girl I have met. She lives in a totally paranoid world, everything she says, everything she *thinks*, is pure fantasy – but she does turn out to have a real live daughter.

BARBARA (*indicating* JODIE). And how on earth did she end up with you?

Throughout the scene, both BARBARA *and* RICHARDS *keep sneaking glances at* JODIE, *an unexpected paternalism/maternalism being aroused.*

RICHARDS. She just threw her at me – she's an extraordinarily scatty young woman . . . (*to* JODIE) isn't she, your mother? (*He smiles.*) An interesting case in many ways, strangely enough it's been rather invigorating meeting her.

BARBARA (*touching* JODIE). I wouldn't queue up to be the child left for you to look after.

RICHARDS (*with surprising intensity*). We *should* have had children.

BARBARA. Oh really? . . . We never seemed to have the time anyway. (*Looking down at the table.*) No that's not the reason – I never felt grown up enough. (*Dark smile.*) And you certainly weren't. Don't know why you mention it now for God's sake anyway! (*Suddenly back at him.*) Why haven't you gone away? You're meant to be having your famous break, disappearing somewhere.

RICHARDS *allows* JODIE *to play on the floor.*

RICHARDS. I have been away – but right here. I've discovered pieces of London – (*self-mocking smile*) that even I didn't know about.

JODIE *toddles up to the glass door, leaning against it. For a moment they don't notice she's gone.*

(*Leaning forward.*) The place – this city – is bulging with forgotten things. Underground tunnels . . . (*he smiles*) tunnels I half knew about of course but had never been curious about, they're stuffed with low-grade secrets, the whole town chockerblock with them, it's underneath, so many things that are hidden with no reason.

BARBARA (*sharp*). Really?

She doesn't recognize the mood RICHARDS *is in. He seems different, like there is a current running through him, constantly moving as he talks.*

JODIE *up against the window, a dark shape is towering above her, the other side of the glass, sheltering momentarily from the rain. It leans down, and opens its case to put something in, revealing strange Masonic robes, strange possessions, the child watches, staring from the dark shape to the case.*

RICHARDS *is moving the butter dish, getting extremely animated, moving everything around the table.*

RICHARDS. If you take a cheese, a bland English cheese, and put it under the microscope it's full of thousands of hidden holes and crawling with insects and bugs.

BARBARA (*watching him*). Next time I think of my cheese like that. . . (*slight smile*) I'll think of you.

The dark shape moves away from the child.

RICHARDS *turns round suddenly, sees the child is not there, shouts:*

RICHARDS. JODIE! JODIE come back here!

JODIE *turns from the window, and* RICHARDS *sees the dark shape, now revealed as a very straight city gent in dark suit, and umbrella, collide with another dark suited city gent, they both exchange apologies and greetings, and scuttle down the back doorway* SHARON *had indicated.*

Maybe those really are masons like she said. (*He touches* JODIE.)

Close shot of a polisher moving across the grubby floor, and then developing to show the cafe now completely empty, the chairs piled high on the tables, their legs in the air, everybody gone except RICHARDS, JODIE *and* BARBARA, *and the girl on the polisher. As the polisher moves across the gunge on the grubby floor, a pattern of fake marble is revealed.*

RICHARDS *talking fast as the polisher whines, there is a new intense quality in his voice, through the dark light.*

. . . but I can't place her, she doesn't fit, lower middle-class background obviously, London, probably Croydon or Bromley, but she isn't easy to categorize, she's a very surprising girl, full of a kind of madness, (*slight smile*) and as you know it's not easy to surprise me.

BARBARA. If you're just going to talk about this lunatic girl for Godsake. (*Pulling at her belongings getting ready to move.*) I can't even get hold of you on the phone for weeks, and suddenly you're desperate to see me, it can't even wait a day, and then *all* you can do. . .

RICHARDS (*stopping her*). No, no . . . I *am* desperate to see you. (*Looking at her.*)

BARBARA *touching* JODIE.

I was thinking, since my holiday in London is now over (*he smiles*), visiting the alternative tourist attractions, I need to go somewhere a little more conventional, (*suddenly looking straight into her face*) this is a terrible way of asking you – I thought we might go away together.

BARBARA. Go away with you! Not so long ago you couldn't bear to be in the same room with me for more than half-an-hour.

RICHARDS (*with force*). No, please . . . I have been thinking differently about us, *re-examining*.

BARBARA. That's good of you.

RICHARDS (*with surprising intensity*). It suddenly seems the obvious course (BARBARA *moves.*) Please listen love. (*Now he is touching* JODIE.) When I used to look back all I could remember was just a sort of smudge, us together, just a claustrophobic blank but (*straight at her*) but it wasn't all like that. (*Pause.*) I have been having the most peculiar dreams about you.

BARBARA (*slight smile*). You'll have to do better than that.

RICHARDS (*more urgently*). I will! (*Almost nervous smile.*) I made an uncharacteristic mess of it. (*Then with real force.*) Please come.

BARBARA. I don't know. I don't trust this sudden intensity, I'm getting a little more used to being on my own . . . I'm not sure I want you barging back in . . . (*Touching* JODIE.) Hadn't you better see to getting your borrowed child back.

RICHARDS (*fondly to* JODIE). Get her back to her batty mother, yes. (*Then turning to* BARBARA *with real feeling.*) Think about it please. I *need* you to come.

Interior – Day

Cut to SHARON *still in the queue of girls, waiting, staring at themselves in the mirror opposite. A voice is saying as they stand there.*

We've had so many application we're not going to be able to get round to everybody – but if you like to hang on in hope, then you're welcome to do so. . .

SHARON'*s fingers beating against the wall.*

Exterior – Day

Cut to RICHARDS *moving along an alleyway in the rain carrying* JODIE *on his shoulder, who is peering about her.*

RICHARDS (*as he moves in the rain*). Jodie don't drop that rattle, not again understood? This is the last time I'm going to ask.

Suddenly two men, HILLCOMBE *and* BOYCE *step out of a doorway, and stand in front of him, barring his way.*

HILLCOMBE *is a plump fleshy man permanently short of breath. Wearing a brown sit, and with heavily ringed fingers. And* BOYCE *is a sandy haired taller man, wearing steel rimmed spectacles.*

They push RICHARDS *up against the wall of the alleyway, as the rain gushes all around them. A building is being rebuilt along the side of the alleyway, and they are surrounded by the scaffolding and flapping pieces of plastic. . .*

RICHARDS *is still holding* JODIE *on his shoulder and is truly astonished at the way he's been accosted. The two men seem totally oblivious of the fact he's holding a child. It's as if they're so pre-occupied with* RICHARDS, *they've completely failed to notice* JODIE, *they jostle him, as they close round him, the child's head going dangerously near pieces of scaffolding.*

HILLCOMBE (*the plump man, who is holding a rolled up copy of the 'Financial Times'*). OK, we've had our fun and games now.

He suddenly flicks RICHARDS' *face with the Financial Times, spiteful little flicks.*

We can all save ourselves an awful lot of trouble – just give it to us now, you won't hear anymore about it, not a whisper, nobody will know you found it!

BOYCE (*barking it out, staccato and loud*). That's a deal. Give it to us *now* – and no more action will be taken. (*Almost shouts.*) None.

HILLCOMBE. So where the hell is it?

RICHARDS. Where's what for Chrissake?

Immediately opposite them in the alleyway is the window of a wine bar, half open. We can hear the noise, shouts and laughter, coming out throughout the whole scene, we can see the bottom half of two peoples' faces laughing, and a hand flicking a cigar on the window ledge.

HILLCOMBE. If you want to play silly buggers, we can play silly buggers.

Rain splashing down all around them.

HILLCOMBE *jerks* RICHARDS' *and* JODIE's *bodies against the wall.*

Where are your car keys?

RICHARDS (*startled*). Car keys?

HILLCOMBE (*shouting*). CAR KEYS! CAR KEYS! Do we have to say everything twice. Your fucking car keys. . .

RICHARDS (*steely*). If you don't let me put the child down now. . .

RICHARDS *watching out of the corner of his eye, the hand flicking the cigar out of the window of the wine bar. Drunken laughter continues to erupt from the window.*

BOYCE (*closing in on him*). What will you do? Hospitalize both of us will you! I think I'll take the chance. . .

BOYCE is suddenly struggling with RICHARDS' pocket, getting the car keys out, he throws them to a third man who has suddenly appeared at the end of the alleyway, and RICHARDS watches in astonishment as he sees his car being driven away.

You won't be seeing that again.

HILLCOMBE (*his voice rising*). But it's not in the car is it! And it's not in the girl's flat!

The 'Financial Times' is now sodden from the rain, he squidges it up in his hand.

(*His voice suddenly leaping higher. We realize he is near panic with frustration.*) Why the hell do you cause us so much TROUBLE.

BOYCE. Gives you pleasure does it, that's what gives writers satisfaction is it?

HILLCOMBE. We have had days of this now. (*His voice really rising.*) *Days* you realize! We had to crawl over every rubbish tip in London before we found you had it! We're *not* going to take anymore! Just give it to us *for Godsake.*

RICHARDS. You mean the bloody film! – is that what you mean?

HILLCOMBE. The film. What film are you talking about? – (*Voice rising.*) Going to a movie are you, is that where you think you're going? (*Loud.*) We're not talking about any fucking film!

He pushes the sodden 'Financial Times' into RICHARDS' face, and twists it round. RICHARDS realises they are in a state of rage and panic which makes them dangerously out of control.

(*As he pushes the paper.*) You know perfectly well what we mean! Going to sell it to the newspapers are we, scoop of the century is it, how much are they giving you? You bloody moron, how could you be so stupid?

He suddenly punches RICHARDS *in the stomach incredibly hard.*
RICHARDS *topples back in the rain, still clutching the child.*

Shot of HILLCOMBE *and* BOYCE *from* JODIE'*s point of view,
in the rain.*

RICHARDS (*as he falls*). You bastards. . .

BOYCE. You've made us look a pair of idiots, something we're
not used to.

HILLCOMBE. It's got to stop! (*Loud.*) Everything to do with you
has got to stop!

BOYCE. If we have to hear your name one more time. . .

RICHARDS *manages to move away from the wall, and puts*
JODIE *down on one of the planks at the bottom of the scaffolding.*
Where she sits, her feet dangling, watching.

RICHARDS. Who are you anyway? You bumbling creeps – you
can't get anything right can you. . .

HILLCOMBE. We could pick you up now, off this street here,
and you wouldn't be heard of again for quite a while, not a
trace – you don't know what we can do in a matter like this!

BOYCE. You've got one more chance mate, and it lasts 30
seconds.

Noise erupting from wine bar.

HILLCOMBE (*frantic*). Just tell us where you put it!

As he says these words he slaps RICHARDS *across the face. The*
violence is perfunctory, spiteful and dangerous.

RICHARDS (*absolutely icy with rage, moving imperceptibly with*
deadly calm). I think what you are looking for, may be right
here. . .

RICHARDS *lets* JODIE'*s bag he has been carrying which is full of*
toys, pour out across the wet ground, the rattles, and hideous knitted
teddy bear.

BOYCE *instinctively bends down to catch the bag as it falls, and as*
he does so RICHARDS *smashes* HILLCOMBE *in the face with*

surprising force, so his plump figure hits the side of the scaffolding and crumples up against a pile of rubbish.

RICHARDS *grabs* JODIE *and sets off down the alleyway. A receding shot of* HILLCOMBE *in a messy fleshy heap.*

BOYCE *stands framed by the flapping plastic sheets and holding the child's rattle.*

BOYCE *makes no attempt to chase after him, he stands watching him go, just moving a few leisurely paces nearer for a better view of* RICHARDS' *retreating figure.*

BOYCE (*calling after him*). There's no point in you doing that. We know where you are all the time.

He moves in the rain still holding the rattle.

We'll see you this evening.

Interior: ANTHONY's *Office Corridors – Day*

RICHARDS *running down a passage, clutching the child. The passage of a large corporation, brown carpets, sleek walls,* RICHARDS *spattered in rain and mud. The comfortable buzz of corporate noise, phones ringing in offices, electric typewriters, all being half-absorbed by the heavy carpets.*

RICHARDS *appears a wild figure in these surroundings. He knocks a trolley of coffee cups as he runs with* JODIE, *sends it spinning in the passage.*

Interior: ANTHONY's *Office – Day*

ANTHONY *in his glass-walled office, separating it from secretaries. Diffused, misty glass and walls, where you can see people pass as out-of-focus shapes. When they stand against the glass peering in, they are merely blurs.*

An expensively furnished office, with some pictures on the walls, a large framed picture of Jane Fonda, and an arty photograph of rocks on an American desert road.

ANTHONY *is fiddling with his individual coffee expresso machine in the corner,* RICHARDS *moving round the office, restless, sharp movements, still blazing from what's happened to him, but his tone is controlled at the beginning of the scene, though he is never still, finding himself momentarily caged in this glass box of an office.*

ANTHONY. I have to stop people stealing my coffee. I have my own private coffee machine – but it is impossible to make the coffee 100% secure.

A blurred shape knocks on the glass door, it is impossible to make out who it is, except that it is probably female.

Who is that? (*Staring at the shape.*) I think it's Diana. (*Shouts waving the shape dismissively away.*) Busy at the moment! In a meeting! Try me later!

ANTHONY *returning to his coffee.*

Now slowly so even I can understand – these people jumped out of the doorway and beat you up – holding a copy of the 'Financial Times'!

JODIE *is sitting on top of the filing cabinet watching everything.*

RICHARDS. Yes.

ANTHONY. And you have no idea who they were? Or why?

RICHARDS (*quiet*). No.

ANTHONY. Incredible. Absolutely incredible. (*Waving.*) And they throw the child at you as well. (*He mimics.*) We've got one spare – so have this!

RICHARDS (*icy*). No, I'll explain later about her.

ANTHONY (*looking at* JODIE). Amazing, isn't it? And what have the police to say about this?

RICHARDS. They told me to go home and they'll find my car for me. (*Murmurs.*) The two comics who attacked me were some sort of police anyway.

Another blurred shape moves up to the glass, about to knock.

ANTHONY (*to himself*). Who's that? (*As shape is about to knock.*) I think it's Jennifer – I quite need to see her. Have we time? No, in a minute. (*Shouting at shape.*) Later Jennifer. I'm in a meeting, try me later love! Very soon.

As shape hesitates and then goes:

I hope it was Jennifer.

He suddenly turns to RICHARDS, *almost aggressively, clearly not wanting him around.*

What are you doing in London anyway? You're meant to be abroad – you shouldn't be here at all!

RICHARDS (*slight smile*). I know it's inconvenient for everyone – but I am here.

ANTHONY. I don't understand what you think I can do. (*Moving away from him.*) Why come to me?

RICHARDS. It seemed the nearest place of 'sanctuary' – in the centre of town. (*Dangerous smile.*) And you always have a good supply of coffee.

A burly brown shape, the shape and size of HILLCOMBE *is moving up to the glass wall, and then pressing himself up to the wall,* RICHARDS *is unaware of it for a moment.*

ANTHONY. Well my advice is – I'm flattered you should want it – go home! (*Slowly as if to an elderly person or child.*) Take the little girl – it is a girl isn't it – take her back to her mother and go home.

RICHARDS (*sharp*). Why there!

ANTHONY *brushing spilt coffee grains back into packet.*

ANTHONY. What do you mean why there!

RICHARDS. Isn't that where they'll be expecting me to go! It's the obvious place, the predictable move.

ANTHONY. Don't be so stupid and paranoid. You've caught a real dose of paranoia from somebody haven't you. (*Indicating* JODIE.) You're planning to keep her for good are you! Like keeping a stray dog, new pet is she!

RICHARDS (*sharp*). Who's that?

He has suddenly noticed the brown shape up against the glass.

Who the hell is that?

ANTHONY. That? (*Peers at shape.*) Not quite sure. Looks like
Barnet. I think it's Barnet. We have a planning meeting
looming you see. (*Shouts at brown shape.*) Just coming, hang on!

Brown shape moves a little.

Pretty sure it's Barnet . . . He must have put on weight.

ANTHONY *moves round office, sharp.*

Now James, I *do* have to get ready you realize – (*Self-
important.*) I have a strategy for this meeting, there's an opening
I want to exploit.

RICHARDS (*watching* ANTHONY *preening at his desk*). I'd
expected you to be a little more surprised, more outraged about
all this. Secret service men beating people up in broad daylight
on the street – used to be quite a favourite topic of yours.

ANTHONY. Quite. But rather more important examples. And
those were different times anyway. This is *London* after all – it's
just a mistake.

RICHARDS (*icy*). Of course.

ANTHONY (*matter-of-fact*). You're quite certain you haven't
acquired something you shouldn't – something they're looking
for. . . ?

RICHARDS *looking at* ANTHONY *moving round his large desk –
his sixties demeanour softened into successful corporate fat.*

RICHARDS (*calmly*). Who's been here Anthony?

ANTHONY (*looking up*). What do you mean?

RICHARDS. Somebody's been round here to interview you
haven't they – about me.

ANTHONY (*immediately defensive, waving his arm*). No, of course
not! I was just guessing, an obvious guess.

RICHARDS *icy calm, moving over to* ANTHONY's *desk, eyes
flicking over the desk, to see if there are any traces, a phone number*

or a card.

What you doing? Don't you dare touch my desk. This is a private area. (*Grabbing armful of paper.*) These papers are confidential! (*Loud.*) Get away from my desk.

RICHARDS. How many came to see you? (*Looking straight at him.*) What did they ask?

ANTHONY (*shouts*). Nobody came.

RICHARDS *stares straight at* ANTHONY's *face, his darting eyes,* RICHARDS *surprised by the extent of the dislike that is welling up inside him.*

RICHARDS. Anthony, you never could lie, could you.

ANTHONY (*sheltering behind desk*). Why don't you go, since you don't seem to feel safe here . . . I have people stacking up outside to see me! I know your work can wait forever – but mine can't!

RICHARDS *moving, dangerous smile, staring at picture of rocks on the American road:*

RICHARDS. Didn't you take this on one of our trips? This load of old stones here?

ANTHONY. No I don't think so. (*Glancing up.*) Maybe you're right, yes.

RICHARDS. Perhaps you should take a better look at it. . .

RICHARDS *suddenly grabs* ANTHONY, *picks him up, sweeping him above his desk, and hangs him on a coat peg by the picture.*

ANTHONY's *short stocky body hanging there.*

(*As he does.*) Been wanting to do this for ages it seems.

ANTHONY (*screams*). James, you've gone crazy . . . (*screams*) completely nuts.

RICHARDS (*as he collects* JODIE *off the filing cabinet, to her, slight smile*). This guy's my oldest friend.

Receding shot as RICHARDS *moves off down the sleek brown passages with* JODIE, ANTHONY's *small gesticulating figure,*

*through the smudged glass, kicking, jerking and shrieking, as one girl
secretary stands outside contemplating* ANTHONY's *jerking
silhouette with a smile.*

Interior: Hairdressing Salon – Day/Evening

Shot of SHARON *sitting marooned, in the half-light, lights turned off
in the salon, the only light is from the office at the end of the passage.*

SHARON *sitting with just one girl left – on a bench – the other girl
making herself up in the mirror in the half-light.*

A voice is shouting at them in the darkness.

VOICE. We're going to just manage I think – because we've
worked so late ourselves – to see you all.

SHARON (*glancing at the other girl*). You have to make yourself
look like Garbo to become a receptionist now.

The clock ticking, SHARON *confined in this cold, mirrored place
looking anxious, staring impatiently about her, but unable to leave if
she wants to have any hope of getting the job.*

Interior: RICHARDS' *Hall and Lounge – Night*

RICHARDS' *house, night just closing in.*

First cut to a series of heavy locks being bolted on the front door.
RICHARDS *making the place secure.*

*He comes in to the main reception room of his house – it has been
searched, all his old books splayed over the floor, some of them ripped
out of their binding. He and* JODIE *stare down at it for a moment.*

Then we cut to RICHARDS, *instead of tidying up adding to the mess,
emptying the contents of his pockets, the waste paper basket, the
drawers, pouring it all over the floor.* JODIE *sitting on sofa watching
him.*

RICHARDS (*staring at the mess*). So they're looking for something
we've got. Let's see if we can do a better job than them. I'm
sure we can! Where is it? What is it Jodie?

We cut to him with all the stuff arranged in neat piles. Camera hovering over the articles, then across his walls, where all the books he has collected, some of them very antique, stare back at him.

Is it one of the books I've collected do you think?

JODIE *is crawling about, off the sofa, onto the floor, picking up some loose change,* RICHARDS *see that.*

RICHARDS *picks up the child, we feel an increasing relationship between them, especially from* RICHARDS.

O.K. – why don't we try this old trick – see what you pick out. You've got as good a chance as anybody.

JODIE *among the piles, crawling about amongst them. She picks out a half-eaten banana – and a parking ticket.*

It was a little silly to try that, I agree.

He reverts to his detached researcher's tone, but he is talking to JODIE.

After all a child of one and a half is less intelligent than a chimpanzee of the same age.

JODIE *picks up the broken necklace of* BARBARA's *that* RICHARDS *pulled out of the incinerator vats, and pushes it into his face.* RICHARDS *smiles at her.*

We cut to RICHARDS *scrunching up a piece of paper and tossing it across the room. There is now a large mountain of scrunched paper in the corner of the room.*

He reaches up to take another piece of loose paper and is about to toss it across the room, when he stops and takes a second look at it.

The camera tracks in, he lays the paper on the floor, and pushes a lamp close so its light floods directly onto it. JODIE *moves near to him too, staring at the paper.*

(*Quiet.*) The medical records, of course.

The camera hovering across the paper.

We see the comments that have been written on this person's medical

*records. We just see odd words, as the camera hovers over the
page . . .*

'COULD PROVE DANGEROUS TO HIMSELF OR
OTHERS' . . . 'SCHIZOPHRENIA' . . . 'COULD COMMIT
ANOTHER SIMILAR ACT'

(*detailed look*). It must be the record of somebody they think
important, Jodie. That must mean a member of the
Government or the Royal Family. . . (*Slight smile.*) I don't think
they'd bother about anyone else. . . (*Turning the paper.*) But
there's no name on the papers we've got is there . . . But they
think I know . . . they think I know the name. (*Louder,*) The
morons must they must have thrown it away by accident . . .
bumbling fools. . .

JODIE *picks up the medical records and runs around the room with
them.*

Interior: RICHARDS' *Bedroom/Landing – Night*

Cut to a shot circling RICHARDS *as he sits at the table with the
medical records in front of him. It is extremely late, just one light on,
the* CHILD *is asleep in a makeshift child-proof area he has concocted.*

RICHARDS *gets up to move to the bathroom. At the very moment he
is about to pull the light cord he hears a loud click downstairs.*

He turns to see JODIE *is wide awake. There is a loud clatter
downstairs, somebody is making no effort to be silent.*

RICHARDS *pulls open the door slightly and peers downstairs.*

Interior: RICHARDS' *Hall – Night*

HILLCOMBE *is in the hall, with the light on, looking at himself in
the mirror, examining the bruise he received earlier in the day . . . At
the same time he is matter-of-factly flicking* RICHARDS' *letters onto
the floor.*

*There is something very disturbing about his total casualness, with the
hall light on, entering the house with insolent ease.*

He then begins to climb the stairs, haul himself up the bannister, puffing and wheezing, looking fleshy but dangerous, in his cheap brown suit. He has surprisingly sharp darting eyes.

He is almost at the top of the stairs when a bleeper alarm goes off on his watch. He immediately stops, turns on the stairs with difficulty, and moves off.

Exterior: RICHARDS' *point of view:* RICHARDS' *Street – Night*

RICHARDS *crosses to the window. Sound of walkie-talkies outside.* HILLCOMBE *is lumbering across the street to a covered van, radios blaring he takes tea and hamburgers off a tray which another man is holding. There are two other dark-suited men standing there, youngish, munching hamburgers and watching the house. A motorcyclist is also there, tall and more menacing, glancing up at the house, smoking.*

RICHARDS *moves across the room and picks up* JODIE.

We cut to him staring down at the addresses of all his friends and acquaintances, shining in green on the screen of his home computer.

RICHARDS. Who do you think we should try to go to? (*He smiles.*) It's not much of a choice is it.

The names stare back at him on the screen. He pushes the erase button.

(*Quiet*). I just lost the address of everybody I know. Why did I do that?

Moving in the darkened room, getting the child ready.

(*calmly*). If your mother wasn't such a lunatic she'd actually possess a telephone. (*Picking up the child.*) I never believed, if I was left alone with a child, I'd burble away to it like this. . .

He crosses over to the window with JODIE, *he sits her on the window sill as they both stare at the men outside.*

Exterior: RICHARDS' *point of view:* RICHARDS' *Street – Night*

He watches HILLCOMBE. RICHARDS *makes one of the sheets of the medical record into a paper dart and throws it out of the window, it circles near* HILLCOMBE, *getting caught in a hedge near him. The men don't notice.*

RICHARDS. Why don't they come in the bastards! They must think I'm not here. I hope. . .

He stares at them, something frightening in their casual disregard.

Are they really stopping just for tea?

Exterior: RICHARDS' *House and Canal – Night*

Cut to RICHARDS, *by the canal, behind the house, moving along through neighbours' gardens, by the dark water, holding the child.*

Cut to RICHARDS *slipping away in a boat along the canal. Boat drifting slowly downstream without engine, as* RICHARDS *stands holding child.*

Exterior: Canal – Night

Cut to the urban part of the North London canal, sliding into the city near Clerkenwell, lit by moon, stark pale light. It is an unsettling scene by night, tall dark walls, old industrial sites, decaying and threatening unusual views that RICHARDS *has never seen before, a gradually increasing, hallucinatory, feeling.*

Exterior: Another Canal Area – Night

Cut to RICHARDS *leaving the boat as it comes to rest at some stone steps.*

Exterior: City Street – Night

He emerges with JODIE *into the city, moving through the night, near Liverpool Street, the National Westminster tower with its red lights blinking, near the Barbican, and the Bank of England with its eerily brightly lit streets, almost as bright as daylight but totally deserted.*

In a key and powerful sequence, he wanders with JODIE *through the City of London at night. As the feeling of being hunted intensifies, so*

RICHARDS *notices things he's never seen before. A hidden, unknown, secretive place seems to reveal itself in front of his eyes. A place he's never seen look like this, a series of quick strong images building all the time.*

RICHARDS *moving through the deserted streets with* JODIE.

RICHARDS. We'll find a cab, we will find a cab eventually.

Headlights appear behind him. A lighted taxi roars down the tunnel near the Barbican and sails straight past him, totally ignoring his attempts to hail it. This happens twice through the sequence, none of them stop for him, and as he gets more frantic, his jerking figure with the child appears more like a weird drunken character.

RICHARDS *passes two dark figures scavenging on one of the derelict sites left in the City, going through the rubble, staring at him as he goes past. One figure hunched under a large black bag.*

The child starts to cry as they move dwarfed by the tall city buildings, the only movement, the old vehicle used by the City to water the window boxes of offices, an old forties lorry that crawls down the street gently spraying the buildings, moving with a sinister slowness.

Cut to RICHARDS *carrying the crying* JODIE, *passing across metal grates in the pavement, pieces of loose paper floating up out of them, or caught in the grates, it's as if the whole place is overflowing with confidential paper, so full, they are erupting out of their underground enclosures.*

He puts the crying child on a low wall, just where a skip is overflowing, papers blowing in the wind.

Don't touch any of it Jodie! We don't want to pick up any other private papers! (*As the child cries.*) My God – the place is deserted. You can't get anywhere in this city at night. (*Shouts.*) Where's the transport!

He sees a man standing dressed for the opera in a doorway of a warehouse, all by himself, staring at him, and a young boy rides by on a bicycle, it has luminous wheels, red and green lights.

Suddenly miraculously a night bus appears at the end of the street, an almost ghostly presence in the city, and comes towards him.

Jesus a bus!

Cut as it looms towards him, he sees it is marked 'Private' it is right on top of him.

RICHARDS *stands waving his arms desperately.*

(yelling). Stop! *(As it roars past him.)* They don't teach people to drive buses at this time of *night!*

Exterior: SHARON'*s Flat and Street – Night*

He reaches the exterior of SHARON'*s apartment, in one of the crumbling old streets on the edge of the East End.*

As RICHARDS *stands with the* CHILD *for a second ringing the bell. He notices a man standing at the end of the street.*

He is surprised to find the man advancing on him. As he realizes SHARON'*s apartment is dark, the man is closing in on him.*

And suddenly RICHARDS *breaks into a real run with the* CHILD *as the man is running, stars to* chase *them, pursuing them, whether out of malice or because he's watching the house* RICHARDS *can't tell.*

RICHARDS *looking back over his shoulder, a very pale expressionless young man hurtling after him down the night streets.*

Exterior: Street on Hill – Night

RICHARDS *runs down a side street.*

He sees a bicycle with its red and green wheels propped against a wall, the boy is relieving himself a little further down the street, with a radio at his feet blasting out into the night air.

RICHARDS *steals the bicycle, somehow managing to hold* JODIE *and pedal at the same time. He sets off downhill on the bicycle.*

RICHARDS *(as he goes).* I'll return it for you at lunchtime!

Cut to a high shot of RICHARDS *on the bicycle with its luminous wheels, holding* JODIE, *pedalling totally alone in the City of London.*

We cut to a fast tracking shot with RICHARDS *on the bicycle moving towards light at the end of an alleyway. A car moves past the mouth of the alleyway, just as he is about to emerge. A battered Mercedes with its windows wound down,* RICHARDS *is startled to see* BOYCE *and* HILLCOMBE *sitting in it, cruising in the night street, looking around them.*

Exterior: Video Factory – Night

Cut to RICHARDS *holding* JODIE, *staring across the street towards the exterior of the video firm, where the party was held. There is one light on.*

He is standing in the shadows, wanting to get across without being seen.

He decides to run straight across with JODIE. JODIE *clinging on for dear life.*

Just as he reaches the other side a voice shouts:

VOICE. What's the hurry?

He turns, it is CURTIS, *in his long coat blinking through his large glasses.*

CURTIS (*grins*). What are you doing round here? Found Sharon's film yet, somebody should! (*He touches* JODIE *and moves off.*) See you around, got to fly!

And he disappears into the night.

Interior: Video Factory – Night

RICHARDS *moves into darkened warren – the dead machines, all switched off. Just one light on in the far corner. As he comes into the main room –* SHARON's *voice comes hurtling out of the dark.*

SHARON. Where've you been? Where the fuck have you been? (*She screams.*) I have been going insane with worry!

She appears out of the dark.

You idiot why didn't you stay where I told you. (*Touching and kissing* JODIE.) I thought something had happened to her. (*Touching* JODIE.) My love.

The extraordinary passion coming out of her after her casual-seeming attitude about her child before.

I came to look for you here. I was about to leave! (*Shouts, beside herself, to* RICHARDS.) Don't you ever listen to what you're told – didn't you think? Have you got no bloody imagination. (*With real force.*) I didn't know where my baby was!

Interior: Video Factory – Night

We cut to SHARON *and* RICHARDS *sitting in the window seat, in the shadows. The whole warren to themselves. The machines gleaming in the half light. Both of them sweating under the low ceiling. They can see down into the street. They are passing a single cigarette between them.* JODIE *is asleep in a corner.*

SHARON (*her head back*). It must be *tiring* knowing everything. . . (*She stretches out the cigarette.*) . . . not being surprised by *anthing* that happens – always expecting it.

RICHARDS *takes drag of cigarette.*

RICHARDS. It must be tiring imagining there is a mystery in the back of every newsreel you see – one could never relax.

Siren ringing in the distance.

SHARON (*calmly*). How can you still think I'm wrong?

RICHARDS. Because you are.

SHARON. People pursuing you all over London and you still think I'm wrong about everything.

Exterior: SHARON's *point of view: Street Below – Night*

She glances down through the window, a motorcyclist is driving down the street below, the cycle moving eerily slowly.

RICHARDS (*smiles*). That was a 'lucky' coincidence, we stumbled upon something else.

SHARON *stares straight at him, her red hair in the dark.*

SHARON. And you didn't even manage to find out *whose* medical records they were! (*Lightly.*) What use are you anyway? (*She looks down into the street.*) Stupid idiots, they threw out something they should keep. So drowning in secrets, they can't remember where the important ones are any more.

SHARON *moving in the dark, she sits in front of the multiple video screens, six blank screens staring back at her.*

The police siren ringing in the distance.

(*Waving towards the siren.*) I don't think that's coming for you by the way – you're not that important.

SHARON *staring at the empty video screens.*

You hate all this don't you? The new tech.

She's watching his reflection in the empty screens as he moves towards her – among the gleaming machines.

You think everything is cheap and predictable now . . . and you don't much like anyone younger than you either.

RICHARDS. *Wrong.* (*Self-mocking smile.*) On what are you basing these wild allegations?

SHARON. You surround yourself with old books.

RICHARDS (*sharp smile moving closer to her all the time*). That's not enough. You can't base such a serious assumption on such slight anecdotal evidence. (*Self-mocking smile.*) Let me teach you something about compiling data. . .

SHARON (*turns on stool, lightly*). But I'm fucking right anyway. (*Jabbing a finger against his shirt.*) It's all hidden away in there. (*Staring up at him.*) I'd say you were bored with life.

Exterior: SHARON'*s point of view: Street Below – Night*

A battered Mercedes moving round the building.

SHARON. Except when you're being chased all over town.

RICHARDS (*staring at her, gently touching her*). Where's the evidence?

SHARON. Also you're wrong about many things, you know.

Moving in the dark, always slipping slightly out of reach.

About my age for instance. I'm *24* . . . I'm not the little girl you thought I was.

RICHARDS (*startled*). I can't have been that much out.

SHARON *switches on the six screens, a leader tape running through them, number counting down on the screen.*

SHARON. You want to know why I'm so 'obsessed' . . . so 'paranoid'. (*Staring at the screens.*) I want to know more that's all. I could say I want to know what to teach her. . . (*indicating the sleeping* JODIE) . . . but I have to teach myself . . . my education being just a little rudimentary – as you've 'delicately' pointed out more than once. (*She switches off tape just as zero appears on screen.*) My history's terrible anyway – so I might as well teach myself my own way. (*Staring at her multiple reflections in the six screens.*) Maybe I see things other people have missed. (*Indicating screens.*) From my training watching these.

RICHARDS (*watching her, lightly*). But your interest is so selective Sharon!

SHARON (*with rather shocking casualness*). That's right – a lot of it leaves me cold.

She throws a tape of 'Swastika' or some other film about the Third Reich across the room.

SHARON *turns to face him.*

But that doesn't make me wrong!

RICHARDS *watching her, wanting to touch her, finding himself incredibly drawn towards her, her febrile unpredictability.*

RICHARDS *by the window, he can see the Mercedes with* HILLCOMBE *and* BOYCE *moving below the window.*

RICHARDS. You know, I've often had a very pleasurable dream, a sort of comfortable nightmare – of being pursued down night streets, being chased through London. . . (*self-mocking smile*) an easy dream to analyse, obviously a banal desire for something else to happen in one's life, to achieve something else. (*Glancing down into the street, he smiles.*) And now it's happened for real, being hunted, I can tell you it's much like I expected. (*He smiles.*) No surprises.

SHARON (*sharp*). Enjoy it while you can, while it lasts.

RICHARDS *staring at her.*

I know what you're thinking – and the answer is *no*.

RICHARDS *gives her a kiss on the nape of her neck.*

Friends. (*Firmly.*) That's what we are. That's more interesting isn't it? (*Slight smile.*) Much less predictable.

RICHARDS (*gentle smile*). I'm getting very fond of you Sharon.

SHARON (*calmly*). Don't let it go further. (*She smiles, a warmth between them*). I'll say this for you – you're not a typical statistician.

RICHARDS. Oh really – and what is a typical statistician like?

SHARON (*gently poking him in the stomach*). Incredibly thin. (*Suddenly her manner sharp again, remembering.*) Apart from anything else, you still think I'm a little mad, certifiable. And that makes me angry. You do, don't you?

RICHARDS (*looking at her*). Yes, just a little.

SHARON (*sharp*). How do I *convince* you?

Angry, looking down into street. A car goes past.

Of course I could always turn you in if I wanted, couldn't I!

Exterior: Tram Tunnel – Night

Cut to CURTIS *moving through the entrance of the tram tunnel, managing to climb the dark fence, and walk down the train rails into the tunnel. Pitch black, the sound of dripping, his torch beam finding the light switch.*

Old electric lights glowing weakly, the tunnel tapering into darkness in front of him. The shape of a vagrant in the darkness, hunched under rubbish in a corner, he looks dead but maybe he's asleep.

CURTIS *moves on, stepping unbothered through the sea of rats droppings towards the wall of black bags piled high at the end of the tunnel, right to the ceiling.*

A wide shot of CURTIS, *a lone figure dwarfed by the pile, moving towards it. He sees no reason to stop when he reaches it, and squeezes through a small gap between bags at the side, forcing his way through.*

On the other side it is pitch black. Just the glow of the light from the other part of the tunnel. A strange noise echoing out of the darkness of the tunnel, maybe wind.

In the beam of his torch we see a pile of dirty rusting film cans.

Interior: Video Factory – Day

Cut to daylight in the warren, in the far distance of the shot we see RICHARDS *asleep in one window,* JODIE *and* SHARON *in another.*

CURTIS *standing in the entrance, moving towards them.*

He puts can of film down in the early morning light, we see the number and title of the film on the rusty can 'HOP PICKING IN KENT'.

We cut to CURTIS, *with the film laced up, switching it on and watching it. He is projecting it on a white wall. The others still asleep, curled up in the windows.*

Stock Shots: Hop Pickers

Stock pictures of hop pickers appear, commentary starts about annual migration to the Kent fields from the grime of London, shots of happy gypsy-like hop pickers, Pathe News-like commentary booming out.

CURTIS *watching the pictures, his attention immediately wandering as he sees what film it really is. He switches on television set to the side of him and starts half watching breakfast television simultaneously, he is moving round on his swivel seat, constant ball of energy and wandering attention, he scrawls a note 'Found this – no interest. Curtis'. A distant*

*phone starts ringing, he gets off his seat, and leaving the film running,
wanders off into the depth of the building to answer the phone.*

*The film is running in the foreground of the shot, and in the background
RICHARDS and SHARON sleeping.*

*We hear the hop pickers commentary and can see the images of the
English countryside.*

*The commentary suddenly cuts out for a few beats as a different image
appears without warning in amongst the hop picking film.*

*A huge close-up of a blonde woman shouting silently on the screen a
disturbing and startling shout.*

The image is over in a flash and the hop picking film returns.

*But then in another few frames there is a close-up of a young man's
face shouting and screaming silently out of the screen, his face covered
in sweat.*
*Another image appears of the blonde woman, she is blindfold. She's in
the middle of the room sitting on a chair. She's swinging her head
round in massive close-up as if people are shouting at her from different
parts of the room. A face in profile appears on the edge of frame
leaning over her. We can see clearly she is a different woman to the one
in SHARON's film. She is imploring the people in the room who we
cannot see.*

*Her face plays in desperate close-up near us, as SHARON and
RICHARDS, oblivious, sleep on in the background of the shot.*

*The images continue to run on silently in the foreground, the woman's
face half turned away from us, unsettling, like out of the depths
somewhere, a darker reality. SHARON and RICHARDS still do not
stir.*

*A reverse shot of the room, RICHARDS' hunched sleeping figure in the
foreground, the black and white images flickering on the screen in the
background.*

*We hear again the commentary on the hop pickers film, suddenly there
is a strange crying noise from the film on the other side of the room, an
inaudible scratchy soundtrack, crackling piercing birdlike noises coming
out of the film.*

We move close on RICHARDS' *face.*

He suddenly wakes, hearing the jarring noise from across the room. The indistinct shouts. He moves over to the film.

Stock Shots: Hop Picking – Day

As he reaches the screen, the hop pickers film returns, and for a few seconds RICHARDS *is staring bewildered at these bland images, searching for the source of the noise.*

But as he stands watching, the images of the young man and woman, shouting silently with startling intensity out of the screen, appear in front of him.

The two of them, the young couple on the screen, are standing in their ordinary forties office clothes, the woman, in a summer dress, standing facing an interrogation, a tribunal, or court of three older men sitting behind a table, high on a dais in a large room, their faces in shadow, one of them is staring down at them waving his arms.

The images are silent, occasionally a weird crackling noise, inaudible shouts and whispers, like a soundtrack is there, lurking somewhere.

The black and white images speed past.

We then see images of the blonde woman sitting in a low chair by herself, turning her head from the camera. And then the young man leans against the wall, his body bent as if he is crying uncontrollably. The black and white film has over-powering close-ups totally unlike an ordinary newsreel, pushing right up close to them.

The shot of the three figures high on the dais. Their faces in shadow. They are sitting straight and formal, like they are passing sentence.

SHARON *has suddenly appeared at his side and is staring at the film.*

SHARON (*quiet*). I told you so . . . I told you so.

RICHARDS (*watching intently*). Maybe.

SHARON (*louder, points at the blonde woman*). But that's not my woman. That's somebody else. That's not her.

RICHARDS. Yes. I know.

He begins to murmur a commentary, an instant reaction, as the film on the screen unfolds.

The camera in the black and white film is moving along a passage, up some stairs, an old dark passage RICHARDS *stares at intently.*

RICHARDS. This is wartime film . . . forties . . . somewhere secret trials being held, detentions . . . a building where this happened, and somebody filmed all this. . .

The camera in the black and white film reaches the end of the passage. A door is opened for it, and it passes into a small room.

The blonde woman is there in the same summer dress, she smiles and jokes when she sees the camera and pulls faces, she is smoking and tries to blow smoke rings as the camera approaches. The camera pans across, the young man is in a new dark suit, and is sitting in the corner, his face more watchful, but he gives the camera a small wave.

The girl leans forward with a smile and breathes into the lens of the camera.

SHARON (*watching the girl's face*). She looks rather nice.

The following shots in the black and white film are startling in their directness.

The camera pans across both the young couples' faces.

Exterior: Back Yard: – Day

There is a baleful shot of a collection of people in a cluster under umbrellas, running in the rain towards the camera.

Interior: Room: – Day

In the next shot the young woman is dead, lying on a floor somewhere.

The camera pushes close towards her, right up to her, her glazed eyes, then moves across the floor to show the boy is also dead, curled up in a heap, in his dark suit.

RICHARDS (*staring quietly*). An execution? They shot them? (*He *watches.*) Maybe suicide. . .

SHARON (*loud*). Who were they?

RICHARDS. They may have been spies . . . suspected enemy
agents . . . who knows? I wonder where this happened.

*There is a series of quick shots of the bodies being covered in sheets,
unexpectedly in floral curtain material.*

Exterior: Back Yard: – Day

*And then the bodies are being carried away across the courtyard, the
carriers carefully avoiding the puddles, they are watched by a clerk
holding an umbrella.*

*There follows an extraordinary shot of the girl's body lying flat on a
table in her summer dress, as two insignificant-looking, round little
men, take her shoes and then her stockings off, preparing the body. The
men are not brutal, their movements are matter-of-fact and respectfully
polite, as they brush her hair away from her face. A change of clothes
for her hangs on the wall behind them. As they begin to cut away her
dress, which has a dark stain on it, we see the boy's body is waiting on
the table behind her. The shots are startling for their intimacy, and the
incongruous, almost surreal image of these two men in neat suits doing
their work and being filmed as they do it.*

SHARON (*fascinated, but at this moment quite detached, staring at
the woman's face*). Is she an office girl – or a major spy?

RICHARDS. Who can have filmed this! What sort of person
could have thought of that? . . . this scene. . .

RICHARDS *is suddenly staring at the table the girl is lying on, at its
heavy legs, for a split moment, we track in on the table, he is staring
very close at it. But the shot then changes.*

Interior: Upstairs Passage: – Day

*The black and white film is moving on, thrusting up some stairs,
moving down a passage.*

The film has suddenly become sharper, more recent looking, a different period. But we are moving down the passages of the same building.

SHARON (*watching, as the film moves*). Where's my woman? Is she in this film at all? What's happened to her? If they've left that bit off. . .

A door suddenly opens in the black and white film, a blaze of light inside. We see people, middle-aged men in the middle of a wild joyous celebration, people waving files, plans at the camera, like an idea has just been given the official go-ahead.

Files marked secret are opened playfully in front of the camera, we see the words 'PROJECT MAGNIFICAT', somebody flips the pages for the camera, we catch glimpses of diagrams, somebody drunkenly adds the words 'very, very, very, etc.' in front of the words secret as the camera watches, the man grinning as he does so. A sense of exhilaration from the whole team, people doing wild and silly things, the footage has a startling quality about it for it has caught people at the precise moment of total unbridled exhilaration and relief.

RICHARDS (*commentary, guessing on the footage*). Champagne . . . a celebration, this is the fifties, we're in the fifties, my father had a suit like that.

People drunk and excited in the film.

A discovery? An idea being born, an invention has just been given the go-ahead? They've just got the news. Maybe this was the birth of some major scientific breakthrough, something extraordinarily important (*he smiles*) – my God they look excited.

Camera moving in on the Project Magnificat file again, the pages flapping open for it.

(*To old film.*) Get closer! (*Instead it moves round the room.*) What was this place? A lot seems to have gone on inside it, where could it have been?

On the black and white film one of the celebrating men beckons the camera towards the cupboard with a broad grin and throws it open, but the image cuts away as we're about to see inside.

There is then a shot of prancing middle-aged figures giving the

thumbs up to the camera and bounding down the passage away from
us before they disappear into the darkness.

Interior: Hall: – Day

The film changes again, the same look for it. Contemporary with the
sequence of the celebration, fifties decor, but a different location, the
main hall of the building.

RICHARDS (*watching, fascinated*). Same period . . . fifties . . .
    maybe the same month.

SHARON (*suddenly points, excited*). *There she is*! It is *her*, isn't it.
    Yes it is! There, see her? The woman in my film.

    SHARON *is pointing to:*

    A shot of a woman sitting alone in the large hall. It is *the woman*
    we have seen earlier in her film.

    She is sitting, her head bent nervously, and then watching, glancing
    around, moving restlessly, she is wearing the same clothes as when
    we saw her before.

    The shot is held from the other side of a large wall, across an
    expanse of floor. Her small figure dwarfed against the wall and high
    windows.

    RICHARDS *is transfixed, staring at something in the shot, just as*
    he was staring at the table, with a sense of recognition.

    He is staring at the expanse of floor.

RICHARDS. Get Jodie. I know where this place is Sharon! (*Quiet,*
    excited.) I know where that is.

    We stay on his face, as he stands staring down at the film with the
    sound of the film running on.

Exterior: London Streets – Day

Shot of them running along dark railings, JODIE being carried. Sleepy
Saturday traffic moving round them.

Interior: The Cafe – Day

The following key sequence intercut with the black and white film, as the old film continues to unfold.

We see the black and white shot of the woman alone in the big room.

We see RICHARDS, SHARON *and* JODIE, *banging through a door into the dark, fading old room that houses the cafeteria where he first had tea with* SHARON. *There is just a* CLEANER *here now. As they come hurrying through the door, they knock over a bucket full of soapy water – as it pours over the floor we recognize it as the same floor as in the room the woman in the film is waiting in. It* is *the same room.*

We cut to the room in the black and white film, the woman moving by the same huge heavy mirror on the wall, but official fifties 'No Smoking' signs are fixed underneath.

We cut back to SHARON *and* RICHARDS.

SHARON (*staring about her*). To say it was under our noses all the time would . . .

RICHARDS. Would be wrong. (*Watching her.*) It was under *your* nose.

SHARON (*turning*) Oh really? *You've* probably passed this building a hundred times. Did you ever wonder about it?

She touches the wall, she is excited, very quiet.

I only came here because the tea was so cheap. . .

SHARON *looks down at the long table, that she and* RICHARDS *had tea at in their first scene together in this place. It is the table the girl's body was on.*

RICHARDS. Yes, it's the same table as in your film. I spotted it.

JODIE *is running her hand across the curved legs of the table.*

SHARON (*staring down*). I know.

They move up to the dusty stairs in the corner. The CLEANER *is shouting after them.*

CLEANER. You can't go up there, it's shut up there. (*Really loud.*) It's shut. And it's private, it's all private up there!

Interior: First Floor Room: Cafe Building – Day

On the next floor they find themselves in an extraordinary fifties time warp, a standard Government sign reminding people of the confidentiality of their work. A room with a couple of posters and pin-ups of the day, Marilyn Monroe, fading picture of Kenneth Moore, and Anthony Eden.

We cut to a black and white film of the woman being guided down a passage by the arm of an unseen man.

We cut to RICHARDS *and* SHARON *moving down the same passage. The building is very affecting, to* RICHARDS, *because of what they have seen in the film,* SHARON's *eyes looking everywhere, drinking in every detail, curious.*

Interior: Ward Room: Cafe Building – Day

We cut to the woman in the black and white film going through the door at the end of the passage and coming into a room with four beds in it.

In each bed is a hideously scarred and injured man, sitting up, propped against pillows. We see the men have not just been badly burnt, the skin is now as healed as it will be, but they're also suffering from mental conditions, a look of distance and fear in their eyes.

They sit in their pyjamas, surrounded by bland fifties decor, an extraordinary and pathetic looking group.

The woman stands staring into the beds for an instant. She recognizes one of the men in the beds.

She moves as if hypnotised, neither looking left nor right, up to the bed he is in, and catches hold of the man with extraordinary passion and longing.

She touches his face, his hair, his lips, seemingly oblivious of his burns and the fact that he only seems to half recognize her, running her fingers along the side of his face and the terrible burns, and then kissing him with a startling intensity.

The camera gets closer and closer recording this immensely private moment, the naked un-English raw emotion, as the woman passionately, uncontrollably kisses and touches the man in the bed.

Suddenly she turns, becomes aware of the camera, she moves towards it, bearing down on it, shouting, pushing her hands towards the lenses, an assault, shouting something desperately over and over again, as the camera moves, the burnt faces watching from the bed, she lunges after it, calling, hurtling straight towards us.

Interior: Former Ward Room: Cafe Building – Day

We cut to SHARON *and* RICHARDS *in the same room with its four decaying beds still there, two of them still have their mattresses.*

All over the walls of the room is the most extraordinary graffiti, drawings and little bits of verse, faces and strange shapes, like out of the subconscious of those that were left in the room. The effect is terrifying but also peculiarly moving.

RICHARDS, (*staring about him, moves close to the strange walls*). It must have been some sort of accident – why they were kept here. Probably one of those very nasty accidents in the early days of atomic power which they hushed up, men caught in a fire in a contaminated area.

Camera moving across the dark weird drawings and graffiti.

Probably this was some sort of secure convalescent unit.

SHARON. Secret.

Interior: Ward Room: Cafe Building – Day

Cut to the woman in black and white film moving about the room, touching the walls, fighting and imploring the cameraman.
We cut back to RICHARDS *stooping to pick up an enamel mug lying, covered in dust, in the middle of the floor.*

RICHARDS. They must have told her, her husband was dead – maybe for months she thought he was dead, maybe for a year.

(*Slight smile.*) For 'security' reasons . . . until the situation was under control.

SHARON *moving by the walls.* JODIE *pushes her hands against a doorway.*

So when people came up to her in the street and said we'll take you to your husband . . .

SHARON *is by the window, staring out into the yard, where we saw the bodies being carried wrapped in curtain material, amongst the puddles. We see in her face, turned away from* RICHARDS *she is beginning to be very affected by this building.*

She turns her head sharply sideways, as if she had heard something humming down the dark passage towards her.

What sort of men could have shot this film? Why on earth did he do it? (*Sharp.*) I don't suppose you find it strange at all. Was it simply voyeurism, was he just bored, or did he think he was making a historical record? He must have dispersed the film deliberately . . .

SHARON *is moving into the darkened opening of the passage, staring into it.*

(*As she moves.*) Hiding it, bits of it, in innocuous Government films, hoping they'd be spotted. Little did he know all the films he chose were going to be classified secret as well! Probably by complete mistake. . .

We are on SHARON's *face, standing staring down the dark passage into the bowels of the building.*

Noise of the black and white film running, growing very loud.

Interior: – Day

We cut into the black and white film, a flow of sharp powerful images, from the depth of the building, coming with a rush, increasing all the time in intensity. Sudden sense of the past of place uncorked and spilling directly at us. Some moments we do not recognize, brief and mysterious, others we see clearly.

We see the celebrating men skipping down the passage, their faces rushing up towards us, the Project Magnificat files almost touching the camera.

We see a handsome, fair haired young man, almost a boy, and a fat old woman together side by side, standing before the three men on the raised dais, as they pass sentence on them. Then we see the faces of the three men on the dais staring directly at us.

We see the girl that died staring into a mirror and doing her hair, a slight private smile coming out of her. We then see her face screaming with pain and then her face dead, right up to the camera, a hand reaches down from the corner of the frame and touches her face, moves it matter-of-factly.

We see a very short man moving towards us down a passage ringing a large bell and grinning broadly, we see a bath entirely full of golf clubs with a girl sitting on the edge looking at the camera, a man in evening dress is glimpsed through a chink in a door sitting alone in his office crying, we see a hunched shape lying in the shadows, a figure shouts down the stairs from the top of the building and sends papers cascading down towards the camera.

We see three women all dressed in black advancing towards us down a passage with pale, expressionless faces. We see a room full of crates and boxes being packed. The last dying days of the building, dead files being thrown into them, we see clearly the Project Magnificat file, being wheeled in front of the camera and tossed into boxes in a section marked 'postponed'.

We see the face of the man who shot the film, in his thirties boyish face with small round glasses, holding a camera and staring manically at us, pointing the camera like a gun, and then the three women in black moving in a totally white empty room, a door opening and they all move away from us.

A noise, a grating squeaking noise, like a voice trying to make itself heard is building in the soundtrack – it is as if the soundtrack is too badly damaged to yield the voice fully but with each shot it gets louder and louder trying to get out.

Suddenly we cut to the woman moving from her husband, the burnt faces staring out of the bland fifties room, as she moves powerfully, straight at the camera.

It is her voice fighting to be heard, as she moves round the room enraged and crying, we hear her voice struggling through the squeaks and distortions, fighting its way out of the past. It is the sound and tone of her voice, full of fury and true passion coming right from her inside, that has the effect on us.

WOMAN. Why didn't you tell me? Oh why. Why was this kept from me . . . *all* this time . . . all . . . didn't you ever think . . . my husband . . . my . . . Why didn't you tell me . . . why . . . why . . . ?

She moves violently across the room, turning her back on the camera, she crosses the room towards the door, the camera follows her.

Exterior: Balcony: Cafe Building – Day

Suddenly with a jarring cut we're with RICHARDS *moving through the same door onto the balcony outside, in the present day, with the red buses blundering past on the Saturday morning streets.*

SHARON *joins* RICHARDS *on the balcony staring down into the streets below.*

RICHARDS *glances back over his shoulder through the door, he has been very affected by the building, genuinely surprised by it.*

RICHARDS. What a place . . . what a curious place.

SHARON *has moved along the balcony, right along, as far as she can go away from us. Her detached manner has gone completely now.* RICHARDS *looks up in surprise to see she is really crying, her body bent against the wall.*

Exterior: London Street – Day

We cut to SHARON, RICHARDS *and* JODIE *walking down sleepy quiet early morning London streets.*

RICHARDS *glancing back, one last look at the building.*

SHARON. It feels it's all over me that building.

RICHARDS. In one's clothes yes.

SHARON (*quiet*). We'll keep the film to ourselves for the moment I think.

RICHARDS *looks at her, she's moving parallel to him, just a little apart.*

RICHARDS (*reaching   his pocket*). I still have some of the medical records, of course. (*He pulls them out.*) Put them back in circulation shall I?

He flicks them with a smile into a dustbin outside a doorway.

Now somebody else can find them on the rubbish tip.

We see we are moving by the dark railings of the Kingsway tunnel, they pass by it.

Interior: Tram Tunnel – Day

We pan back for a moment along the railings and then cut inside the tunnel where the old man who looks after the tunnel is sweeping up along the dead tram lines while confidential papers flutter around him.

Exterior: London Square – Day

We cut back to RICHARDS and SHARON moving across a large empty London square. JODIE pulls at a piece of printed paper that is fluttering, caught in a railing, she tears at it, trying to get it free of the railing.

SHARON (*quiet, moving the child*). Don't touch Jodie – we're not ready, we're not starting again.

RICHARDS. Not just yet.

SHARON *looks at him in surprise.*

SHARON (*she smiles*). You've got a taste for it now have you.

RICHARDS. Maybe.

SHARON (*calmly*). You'll probably become worse than me. About all this.

High shot of them moving across the square, surrounded by large buildings.

They are both staring around them into London.

It looks different now doesn't it.

RICHARDS (*staring about him at the City*). Yes . . . (*Forcefully.*) Yes it does.

He continues to stare about him, as he walks, at the different City.

Interior: Tram Tunnel – Day

We cut back to the little man in the tunnel, sweeping away, the papers fluttering all around across the floor near him.

He picks some of them up, they are the confidential menus of the long forgotten Royal Banquet, sole Bonne Femme, followed by Boeuf Wellington, he puts them back in their place.

We pan across from there to what's next to him, sticking out of the top of a crumbling old box, covered in dust, with a couple of small beetles crawling over them, are the files of PROJECT MAGNIFICAT staring back at us.

Credits

As the titles roll on one side of the screen, the flickering black and white image of the woman in the film looking back at us, and then moving through a door at the end of a room and disappearing into darkness.